eBay - Tweaks, Tips and Tricks

Robert Penfold

Bernard Babani (publishing) Ltd
The Grampians
Shepherds Bush Road
London W6 7NF
England

www.babanibooks.com

Please note

Although every care has been taken with the production of this book to ensure that all information is correct at the time of writing and that any projects, designs, modifications, and/or programs, etc., contained herewith, operate in a correct and safe manner and also that any components specified are normally available in Great Britain, the Publisher and Author do not accept responsibility in any way for the failure (including fault in design) of any projects, design, modification, or program to work correctly or to cause damage to any equipment that it may be connected to or used in conjunction with, or in respect of any other damage or injury that may be caused, nor do the Publishers accept responsibility in any way for the failure to obtain specified components.

Notice is also given that if any equipment that is still under warranty is modified in any way or used or connected with home-built equipment then that warranty may be void.

© 2011 BERNARD BABANI (publishing) LTD

First Published - April 2011

British Library Cataloguing in Publication Data
A catalogue record for this book is available from the British Library

ISBN   978 0 85934 716 7

Cover Design by Gregor Arthur
Printed and bound in Great Britain for Bernard Babani (publishing) Ltd

Preface

It is now many years since the dot-com "bubble" burst, and numerous Internet based companies that were previously valued at millions of pounds became severely devalued, or even disappeared altogether. There were some exceptions to the crash, and a few of these Internet survivors not only managed to stay in business, but actually grew into vast companies. In fact one or two became household names, and are amongst the best known companies in the world.

EBay certainly falls into this category, and seems to have grown steadily over the years, with a stream of new sites being opened in countries around the world. For many people it is now the first place they look when they wish to buy new or second-hand goods, and it provides the best chance of locating many types of rare collectable items. In fact it is a "dream come true" for many collectors around the world. You are not restricted to trading within your own country, and many eBay users now buy and sell internationally.

Although it is still regarded as an auction site, the majority of sales on eBay are for fixed priced goods, and auctions are now in the minority. You can buy goods on eBay much as you would from an online retailer. In fact many online retailers use eBay as an addition to or instead of their own web site. However, for most private eBay users it is the auctions for second-hand and collectable goods that are the most interesting, and it is these that attract most new users. EBay has made trading via their sites more straightforward than it used to be, but there are still a number of pitfalls that new users need to be aware of.

It has to be emphasised that this book is not intended to be a "get rich quick" guide. No doubt much of the information contained herein would be helpful to professional eBay users, but this is not the main aim. I am a camera collector, and this book is a digest of lessons learned while buying and selling photographic items on eBay over the last ten years. During that time I have bought and sold a few thousand items via eBay. This book is designed to help private eBay users make the most of the site when buying or selling. It will help you to find the items you wish to buy, get the best price when buying or selling items, put a realistic valuation on items for sale, avoid mistakes that can result in your items selling for a fraction of their true market value, and avoid scams. It is effectively a catalogue of things I wish I had known before I started. I learned the hard way, but there is no need for you to follow suit!

Robert Penfold

Trademarks

Microsoft, Windows, Windows XP, Windows Vista and Windows 7 are either registered trademarks or trademarks of Microsoft Corporation. eBay.co.uk, eBay.com, and PayPal are registered trademarks or trademarks of eBay Inc.

All other brand and product names used in this book are recognised trademarks, or registered trademarks of their respective companies. There is no intent to use any trademarks generically and readers should investigate ownership of a trademark before using it for any purpose.

Contents

1
EBay buying 1

EBay buying 1
Getting carried away 2
Remember the postage charge 2
Multiple items 3
Avoid high postage 3
Postage fraud 4
Typical bidding pattern 4
Sniping 5
Sniping flaw 5
Inconvenient sniping 6
Timed sniping 7
EBay toolbars/sidebars 7
Automated sniping 9
Reliability 11
Practical software 13
Currencies 14
Lead time 16
Pro version 18
Keeping track 23
Group bidding 25
Online bidding sites 28
Using Goofbay 29
Sniping Button 35
Shill bidding 38
Use PayPal 39
Nearly new bargains? 40
Second chance offers 40
Risky bargains 41
No photograph 42
Terrible photograph 42
Photo processing 43
Reserve price 44
High Buy-it-Now price 45
Low feedback 45

Wrong category 45
Buying from abroad 46
Understand the description 47
Translation 47

2

Selling on eBay 51

EBay selling 51
Photographs 51
Camera 53
Film camera? 53
Scanning 54
Sections 54
Heading 55
Description 56
Starting price 57
Using a low start 57
The right price 59
Rare commodities 60
Do not get conned 61
Dubious offers 61
Make Offer button 62
Piece by piece 63
Current value 64
Breaking up 65
Boxing clever 65
Searching 66
Completed listings 67
Search types 68
Sort by 71
Matching mistakes 72
Erase personal data 74
Personal collection only 77
Secure packing 77
Phone home 78
Stick by the rules 79
Selling abroad 79

3
Photographs for eBay 81

Good photographs 81
Taking photographs 81
Avoid backlighting 83
Avoid camera shake 84
Using flash 86
Fill-in flash 90
Diffuser 93
Close-ups (macro) 94
Digital zoom 94
Fill the frame 96
Keep it clean 96
Correct focus 97
Correct exposure 98
Flash compensation 99
How many pictures? 99
The right one 100
Processing 101
Cropping 102
Exposure adjustment 103
Shadow/fill-in 104
Off colour 104
Straight and narrow 105
Resizing 106

4
Everyday eBay 107

Avoiding scams 107
When to send 108
Cash on collection 108
Money transfer 108
Feedback blackmail 109
eBay phishing 109
Spoof eBay emails 110

The box	110
Fake feedback	111
Short duration auctions	112
Dealing off eBay	113
Mystery postage	113
Problems, problems	114
Dispute resolution	114
Shifting goalposts	115
Be patient	115
Stick to the rules	116
My eBay	116
Customise	118
Index	119

1
eBay buying

eBay buying

Buying goods on eBay is much easier than selling them, and you can get started almost straight away. You have to register an account with eBay, but you can then start bidding, or buying goods in a so-called "fixed price" auction. This is a contradiction of terms if ever there was one, as a fixed price auction is an auction where there is no bidding. Instead the listing has a Buy-it-Now button, and you can use this to buy the goods immediately. In other words, the goods are sold via what is really just an ordinary advertisement. Sometimes the Buy-it-Now option is included as part of a normal auction listing, giving the options of bidding or buying straight away.

With this type of auction the Buy-it-Now option disappears when the first bid is placed, or when the reserve price is reached if the seller has set a reserve on the item. In most cases this means that the Buy-it-Now option disappears if you place a bid, but this is not necessarily the case if there is a reserve price. You might lose the item if you are outbid in the normal way, or someone could use the Buy-it-Now option, thus ending the auction. Note that sellers can state the reserve price on their listings, but few actually do so. Few will reveal the price if you ask them to do so using the eBay messaging facility. It can be useful to remember that the minimum reserve price on an eBay.co.uk auction is fifty pounds.

There is a variation on the standard version of a fixed price auction, and this is the inclusion of a facility that enables an offer to be sent to the seller. Depending on how the seller has set up the listing, an offer will be automatically accepted or declined, or sent to the seller for their consideration. The listing remains active if your offer is sent to the seller, and it is not put "on hold" until the seller reaches a decision. If someone uses the Buy-it-Now option during this time your offer is automatically declined and the listing closes. Others can make offers while yours is being considered, and once again, your offer is automatically declined and the listing closes if the seller accepts a better offer. Offers expire after 48 hours should the seller fail to reply to your offer. Buy-it-Now sales of one type or another apparently constitute slightly more than half of the total sales on eBay, so it would be wrong to think of eBay purely as an auction site. Vast amounts of new and second-hand goods are sold using the fixed price auction method, or one of its variants.

Getting carried away

I was listening to the radio some time ago when one of the Radio 5 Live presenters stated that she was a typical eBay "newbie", and after opening an account had immediately bought several cars! She then had to explain to the sellers that she did not actually want the cars, and had to rely on their understanding to get her "off the hook". I think that she was not really typical of newcomers to eBay, but there was an element of truth in what she said. There is a temptation to bid on things "left right, and centre" without thinking things through properly. When you bid on an eBay auction or use a Buy-it-Now option you are entering into a legally binding contract. While it is unlikely that anyone would sue if you failed to go through with the purchase of an item you won on eBay, this is a situation you should never get into in the first place. For one thing, you could soon find yourself banned from eBay if you win items and do not pay for them.

Only bid on something if you are prepared to go ahead and complete the deal at the price you bid. Do not bid on something in haste, look at the listing again later, and then realise you have bid far too much. Before you bid, check that the item is the exact one you required, that you are satisfied with its condition, that it is complete with any vital accessories, and that it is genuinely worth your intended bid price. It would be a mistake not to bid on something because there are one or two vital accessories missing, but you should check that the missing parts can be obtained, and the bid price should be adjusted downwards to allow for the cost and inconvenience of having to obtain them separately.

Remember the postage charge

You may occasionally buy something where it is a practical proposition to go and collect it in person, but in most cases the goods will have to be posted to you. The cost of postage should be deducted from the total price you are prepared to pay, and that is the price you should bid. These days the postage charge is usually quoted in the listing, but if necessary, check the cost with the seller before bidding.

Multiple items

Another classic beginners' mistake is to search for something, find several listings with items that match your requirements, and then place bids on all of them. In this situation it is possible that none of the bids will be successful, or that only one will succeed and that you will buy the item you need. However, there is a likelihood that you will end up winning two or more items, and you will then be expected to go ahead and buy all of them! Failing to do so could get you banned from eBay. Placing bids on several items and then trying to retract bids when you win one of them is not an acceptable way of doing things either. Again, it is a practice that is likely to get you banned from eBay sooner rather than later. The right way of going about things is to place a bid on the auction that will end first. If you are unsuccessful, repeat the process, and keep bidding on the auction that will end soonest until you win the item or admit defeat and give up. At one time there was a facility built into eBay that largely automated this type of bidding process, but it seems to have been withdrawn due to lack of use. There is certainly third party software that achieves much the same thing, but I prefer to take personal control of the bidding process. This encourages a more careful and less cavalier approach.

Avoid high postage

Postage rates for the same item vary enormously. Sometimes there are good reasons for this, and the postage for something like a camera with no accessories is likely to be less than for the same camera that comes complete with its original box, instruction manual, software discs, battery, a battery charger, and several leads. Some sellers subsidise the postage cost in the interests of good customer relations, while others charge the full cost of postages and the packaging materials. Others try to make a profit on the postage charges, and in some cases the postage charge is completely "over the top".

One reason for sellers using high postage costs is to avoid paying most of the final listing fee. The seller pays a final listing fee that is a certain percentage of the selling price. The percentage varies, but is usually ten percent for non-business users. Buyers do not pay any eBay fees incidentally. If an item sells for two pounds and the postage charge is fifteen pounds, the final listing fee is very low as it is based on the selling price of two pounds. If an item sells for fifteen pounds and the postage charge is two pounds, the final value fee is relatively high because it is based on the higher selling price of fifteen pounds. The amount received by the seller is the same in both cases, at a total of seventeen pounds.

Postage fraud

Another reason for a high postage charge being used is to deliberately defraud the buyer. In such cases the goods being sold are faulty or of inferior quality. The buyer will probably demand a refund, and in all probability will get one. However, most sellers will only refund the purchase price, and will not pay for any postage costs when an item is returned, regardless of the reason for its return. In the example given previously, the seller would keep the fifteen pound postage charge and refund the two pounds paid for the item. Having paid the return postage plus the original postage change, the buyer is about seventeen pounds out of pocket. Meanwhile, the seller still has about fifteen pounds minus some eBay costs. In other words, the seller has made nearly fifteen pounds for selling nothing!

eBay has taken some steps to prevent excessive postage charges, but it is practically impossible to eliminate this practice without placing undue restrictions on sellers. It is therefore something that you might encounter from time to time. Anyone indulging in this ploy is at best less than completely honest, and at worst is a fraudster. Experienced eBay users have nothing to do with any items that have clearly excessive postage charges, and you would be well advised to follow the same tenet.

Typical bidding pattern

If you watch how the bidding progresses on a few items you might find that things develop much as you would expect, with bids being made at intervals, and the price steadily building until the closing time and date of the auction is reached. In other words, the bidding proceeds in a similar fashion to a conventional auction. In the early stages there are bids and counter bids from bargain hunters, with the serious bidders only coming in near the end. Everything is at a much slower pace of course, because the auction will typically run for one week, and it cannot last for less than one day. Note that, unlike some other online auctions, eBay auctions are not extended if a bid is placed close to the closing time.

This is a crucial point in explaining why many auctions do not proceed in the manner described above. With very popular items it is quite possible that things will indeed develop in the expected fashion, and the final price might actually be reached well before the auction's end. A more common scenario is that there is very little bidding initially, with most of the bids being placed just before the auction closes. In many cases the serious bids are placed in the last ten seconds or so of the auction! This can be partially explained by people placing a bid on one item, and then moving on the next item of that type if they do not win the first one. This process of waiting for one item to end before moving on to the next tends to produce late bidding, but it does not really explain the sudden rush of bids on the last few seconds.

Sniping

The rush of bids at the end of many auctions is due to a practice known as "sniping", which is deliberately waiting until the auction is about to close before placing a bid. The main idea of this bidding in the last few seconds is that it does not give your competitors any time to have a change of mind and increase their bid. If you place a bid at the maximum price you are prepared to pay when an auction still has several days to run, it is quite likely that someone will place a bid that is a little lower than your bid. If they place the bid when the auction still has hours or days to run, it is quite possible that they will give in to temptation and place a higher bid before the end of the auction, possibly beating your bid with this second attempt. In fact they might place three or four bids, with a winning bid eventually being placed. This cannot happen if you place your bid about five seconds before the end of the auction. Even if your rival bidder is watching the final stages of the auction and he or she decides to place a higher bid, they will probably not have time to place another bid before the auction ends.

Sniping flaw

You do need to be aware of a potential flaw in sniping, which is that the eBay bidding system does not always operate in a fast and efficient manner. Possibly due to high demand on the eBay server, or perhaps due to a bottleneck on the Internet, it can sometimes take a while to place a bid. If you try to place a bid ten seconds from the end of the auction you might fail to get in a bid at all. A temporary blockage in the Internet or a problem with your PC could produce the same result. When bidding on something that is particularly important to you it is probably best to place your bid half a minute or more before the auction closes, rather than leaving it until the last few seconds.

1   EBay buying

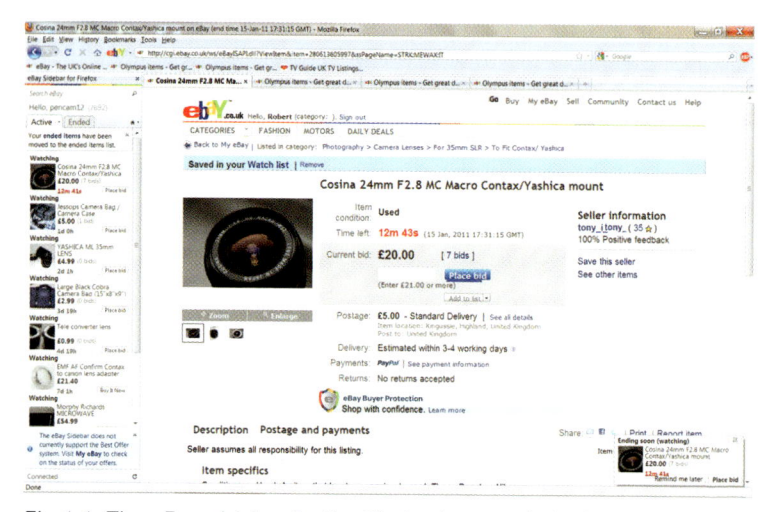

Fig.1.1 The eBay sidebar for the Firefox browser is in the left-hand column. An alert has been generated and is displayed in the bottom right-hand corner

Inconvenient sniping

An obvious problem with sniping is that you have to be at your computer, signed into eBay, and ready to bid on the item just before the auction ends, whatever day and time of day that happens to be. To say the least, this is not a particularly convenient way of doing things. Most auctions end at a reasonable time rather than in the middle of the night, but there are exceptions.

I do not claim to understand the reasons for some European sellers having listings that end at about 3.00 in the morning, but some do end at times when most of us are asleep. Possibly some of the offending sellers have used the facility that enables the auction to be started at a chosen time and date rather than as soon as the listing process has been completed, and they have selected an AM time instead of a PM one in error. If you bid on auctions for items outside Europe it is only to be expected that many of them will end in the early hours of the morning in the UK. Anyway, sniping will not be a practical proposition with some auctions, and it is then a matter of placing your bid as close to the end of the auction as you reasonably can.

EBay buying 1

Fig.1.2 The sidebar will still function if you move to another website

Timed sniping

A less obvious problem with sniping is that most of us in the modern world are very busy and it is easy to become distracted so that you forget to place a bid. I have to admit that I have missed the ends of numerous auctions in this way, and have probably missed a number of good buys as a result. One solution is to simply use an alarm clock to provide a reminder a few minutes before each auction ends. In fact these days there are numerous alternatives to an ordinary alarm clock, and it is possible to obtain small pocket timers that can sound an alarm after a certain time has passed or when a certain time has been reached. Many wrist watches have an alarm facility, or this feature might be available from your mobile telephone. It does not really matter too much which method is used, any gadget that provides an alert just before an auction ends could prevent a lot of missed opportunities.

EBay toolbars/sidebars

There are several eBay add-ons for the popular web browsers such as Internet Explorer and Firefox, and these often include an alert facility that warns you when an auction that is being watched on your My eBay page is about to end. The one shown in the example of Figure 1.1 is the eBay

1   EBay buying

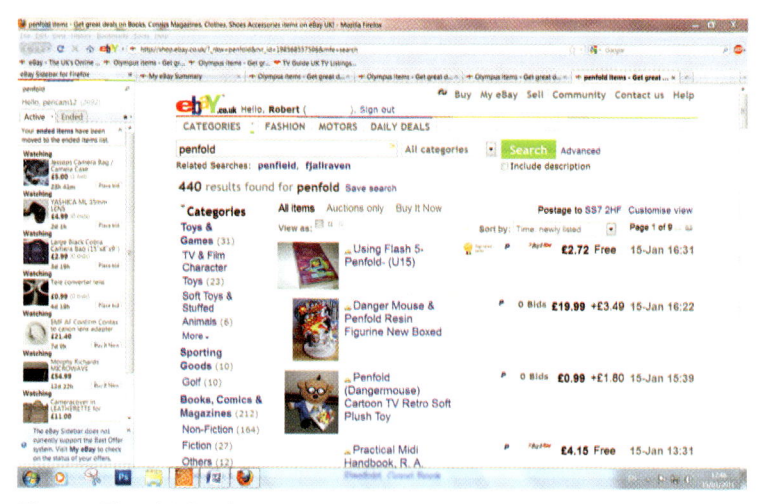

Fig.1.3 The sidebar includes a search facility

sidebar that is available for Firefox. Any good search engine should soon locate this one, and probably a few other eBay add-ons for Firefox as well.

The main section of the sidebar is used to show the items on your watch-list that will end the soonest. The time until the end of the auction is displayed in real-time for any auction that has under one hour left to run, just as it is when viewing the full page for a listing. This makes it easy to monitor the time you have left before a bid must be entered for an auction. The sidebar can also generate alerts as the end of the auction gets close, and in this example a small alert window can be seen near the bottom right-hand corner of the page.

It is not necessary to have the page for a listing loaded into one of the tabs in order to use the sidebar, and it is not even necessary to have an eBay page of some sort loaded into one of the tabs. You can carry on surfing on other sites (Figure 1.2) and the sidebar will still function normally. Obviously you must sign into eBay using the right browser before the sidebar can function, and you must remain logged into eBay while the sidebar is in use, but nothing more is required in order to use it. The sidebar seems to place minimal loading on the computer's resources. A simple eBay Search facility is available using the textbox at the top of the sidebar (Figure 1.3).   The Ended tab below this enables the sidebar to be switched to show the watched listings that have ended recently.

This provides a quick way of checking to see if you have won an auction that has just ended.

An obvious drawback of a sidebar or toolbar add-on is that it occupies a significant area of the screen, although with modern computer video systems the resolution is high enough for this to be of minor practical significance. Anyway, it is not essential to have the sidebar on the screen in order to use the alert facility. This will still work provided the browser is running and you are signed in to eBay. The little alert window will appear in the normal way if you are using the browser, or an alert will be generated via the taskbar if the browser is minimised.

The main problem in my experience is that you can still miss the end of an auction. In this example I did bid in the last few seconds and win the item at a good price, but I have sometimes missed out when using sidebar and toolbar add-ons. The eBay add-ons work well provided you are working at the computer, but if you move away from the computer they become of little use, especially if you move well away from the computer. You can take a small timer and alarm unit wherever you go, and it will still be effective if you move into another room, or pop next door.

Automated sniping

A more sophisticated approach to sniping is to use software to automatically place bids just before the end of an auction. There are two ways in which this can be done, and one of these is to have a sniping program running on your computer. This is an extension of the eBay sidebar or toolbar idea, where the software not only monitors items on a watch list, but also places a bid at the required price and time.

This is the preferred method for some because it does not require you to divulge your eBay login details to a third party. The drawback of this method is that your PC must be switched on and running at the times when bids must be placed. Depending on the type of computer you use, this may or may not boost your electricity bill if it means leaving the computer switched on for long periods so that the software can place bids.

It should be noted that leaving a computer running and unattended for any length of time should be avoided, as it constitutes a fire risk. Another point to bear in mind is that things might not work as expected if you set everything up and then leave the computer to get on with the bidding. The likely outcome is that on returning to the computer you will find that it is in Standby mode and has not placed any bids. For this type of thing

1 EBay buying

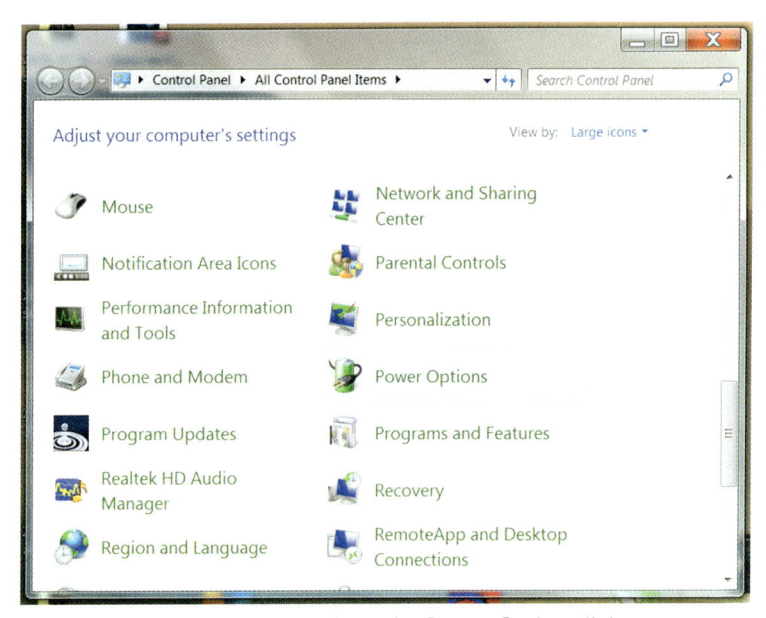

Fig.1.4 Scroll down to and activate the Power Options link

to work properly it is essential to set the computer's power settings so that it does not go into any form of Sleep or Standby mode even if it is left running but untouched for a long period of time.

In Windows 7 this can be achieved via the Power Management section of the Windows Control Panel. The Control Panel can be launched by going to the Start menu and choosing the Control Panel option, which should be in the right-hand section of the menu. Select either the Large Icons or Small icons view from the drop-down menu near the top right-hand corner of the window, and then scroll down to the Power Options icon (Figure 1.4). Left-click the Power Options icon or the text link, and in the new version of the window left-click the Change Plan Setting link for whichever power management plan is currently in use. In the new version of the Control Panel window there will be a "Put the computer to sleep" menu, and here the Never option should be selected (Figure 1.5).

The other menu controls the delay between the last time the keyboard and mouse was operated and the screen being switched off. Provided the computer is not in any form of Sleep or Standby mode, it should still operate normally in the background even if the screen is switched off.

EBay buying 1

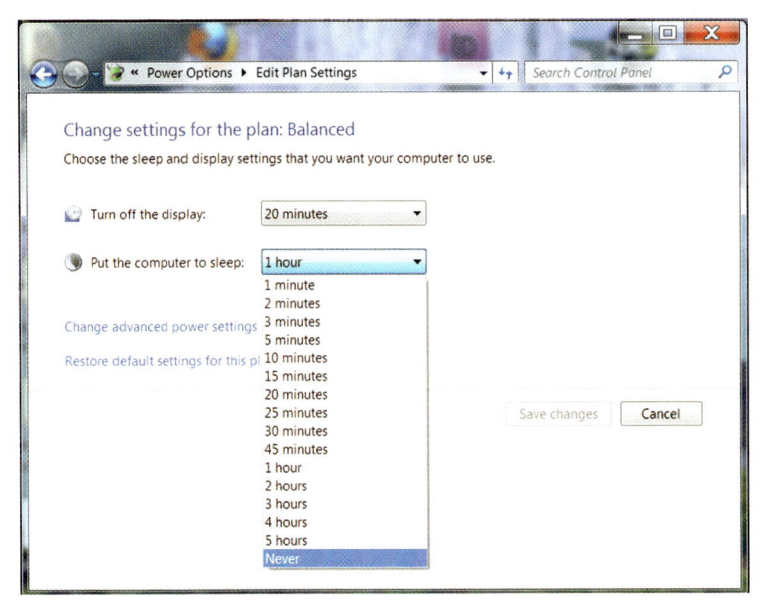

Fig.1.5 Select the Never option from this menu

Consequently, it should not be necessary to use the Never option here as well, although in use you might find it more convenient to do so.

Reliability

When using any form of automated bidding you have to bear in mind that it is likely to be something less than one hundred percent reliable. As already pointed out, when sniping manually it is possible that from time-to-time there will be a hold-up somewhere in the system that will prevent your bid from being placed in time. The closer to the end of the auction a bid is placed, the greater the risk of it going through too late to be accepted. The same is true of automated sniping. The risk is exactly the same whether using sniping software running on your computer or placing an equivalent bid manually. In both cases the bid is being made from the same PC, and through the same Internet connection. Presumably the same Internet infrastructure will also be used, and the bid will be handled in the same way by the eBay server.

The situation is different when using a sniping service where the bids are made from the equipment of the service provider. The risk is probably

1 EBay buying

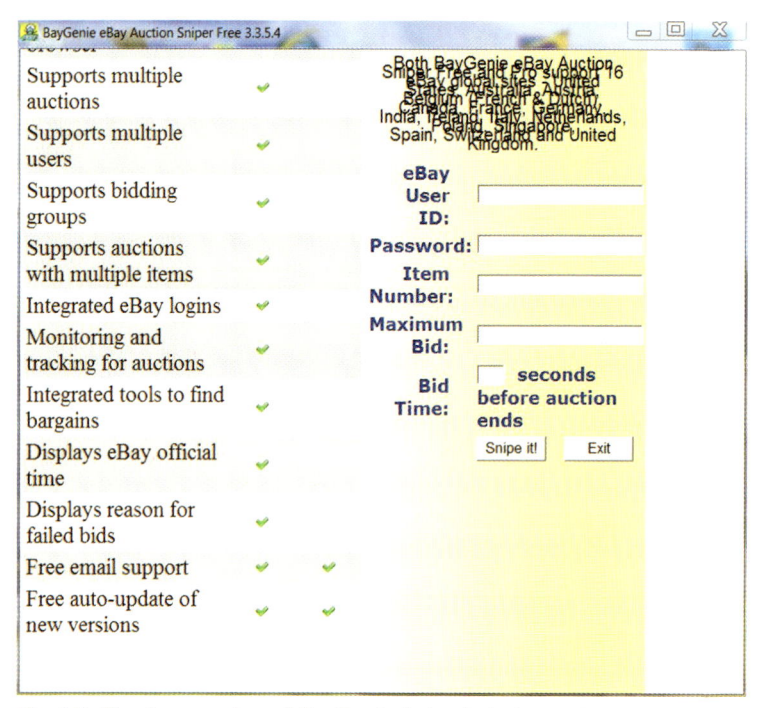

Supports multiple auctions	✔	
Supports multiple users	✔	
Supports bidding groups	✔	
Supports auctions with multiple items	✔	
Integrated eBay logins	✔	
Monitoring and tracking for auctions	✔	
Integrated tools to find bargains	✔	
Displays eBay official time	✔	
Displays reason for failed bids	✔	
Free email support	✔	✔
Free auto-update of new versions	✔	✔

Fig.1.6 The free version of BayGenie is basic but easy to use

much the same with a basic service of this type. Due to geographical differences it is possible that a bid that would have succeeded if placed from your own computer will fail when placed by the service provider. However, the opposite is also true, and there could be a few bids that would have succeeded if placed by the service provider, but will fail when placed from your computer. Overall, it is unlikely that one method would provide better reliability than the other.

Some service providers try to provide improved reliability by using multiple servers, but the claimed success rate is still usually a little short of one hundred percent. It is difficult to see how perfect reliability could be obtained via the Internet, which is not itself totally reliable. A bid should be placed manually well before the end of the auction if you need to be completely sure that it will be placed successfully. If there is a problem, you can keep trying until the bid does go through the system successfully.

EBay buying 1

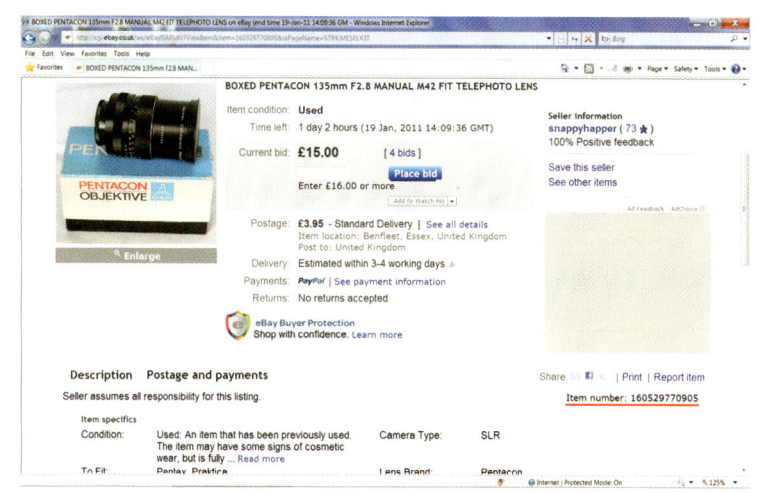

Fig.1.7 The eBay item number is shown on the listing page. Here it is towards the bottom-right and has been underlined in red

Practical software

There are free versions available for both types of automatic sniping, but as one would probably expect, the free versions tend to be limited in scope. BayGenie is one of the best known pieces of sniping software, and it exists in a basic version that is free, and a paid for "Pro" version. With automatic sniping services it is only to be expected that a subscription is normally paid, rather than a one-off payment "up front". Automatic sniping software often works in the same way, and there is (say) an annual licence fee to pay in addition to the initial purchase price. This is the method used with the Pro version of BayGenie.

The free version of BayGenie (Figure 1.6) is, to say the least, extremely basic, but it does provide an easy way of setting up automatic snipes on a one-by-one basis. On running this software you must scroll down to the bottom of the page, and here you must first enter your eBay user ID and password. This information is required with any system of automatic sniping so that the software can log into your account and place bids.

The user Interface of BayGenie Free is very basic, and the only way of indicating which item you wish to bid for is to enter its listing number into the appropriate textbox. The item number seems to be somewhat less prominent on the listing page than it used to be, but it is usually to be

1 EBay buying

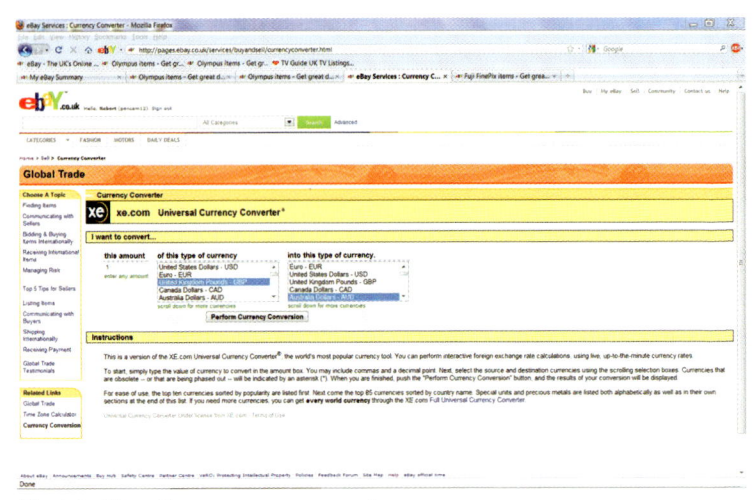

Fig.1.8 The eBay currency converter page

found below the main heading section on the right-hand side. It is underlined in red in the example shown in Figure 1.7. This can be copied and pasted into the textbox using the computer's normal Copy and Paste facilities.

Currencies

The maximum price you are prepared to pay for the item is entered in the Maximum Bid textbox, and as always when entering a bid, you must be careful to avoid errors. Avoid falling foul of the classic errors here. In particular, bear in mind that you will be bidding in the currency used in the listing, which might be different to your home currency if the listing has been placed by someone in another country. It will almost certainly be different if you bid on items listed on eBay sites outside your own country.

EBay has some built-in help, and by default it will provide a conversion of the current price or Buy-it-Now price to your local currency. There is no automatic help if you bid on items listed on eBay sites outside your home country, but there are plenty of web sites that can provide various types of currency converter. There is actually an eBay currency converter, which operates in conjunction with an external web site. The easiest

EBay buying

Fig.1.9 The menus are used to select "to" and "from" currencies

way to go to the appropriate page of eBay is to enter "currency converter" into the eBay Help system, and this should provide a link to the page.

The currency converter page is shown in Figure 1.8, and a zoomed view of the important part of the page is shown in Figure 1.9. Using the

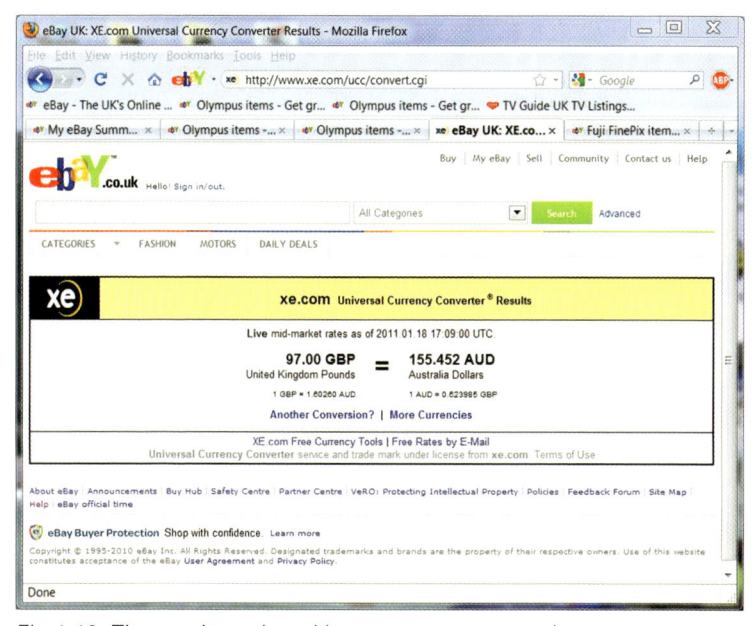

Fig.1.10 The result produced by a currency conversion

1   EBay buying

converter is just a matter of choosing your local currency from the left-hand menu, entering the appropriate amount in the small textbox, selecting the currency used in the auction from the right-hand menu, and then operating the Perform Currency Conversion button. After a short delay the result of the conversion will be displayed (Figure 1.10). It is advisable to perform a conversion in the opposite direction to find the cost of postage and packing in your local currency. Unfortunately, the cost of international postage is often so high that there is no point in bidding on the item.

An important point to keep in mind is that the amount you pay will not be based on the conversion rate at the time your bid is placed. It will be based on the conversion rate at the time you pay, and assuming that payment is made using PayPal, it is the PayPal conversion rate that will be used. Currencies rise and fall in value, and this can work in your favour or against you, but it is prudent to allow for the fact that the final cost of buying an item can be several percent higher than you originally expected.

Lead time

Returning to BayGenie and Figure 1.6, a time in seconds is entered in the Bid Time textbox. If you enter a time of (say) ten seconds here, the program will try to place your bid ten seconds before the end of the auction. As always with auction sniping, leaving the bidding until almost the end of the auction ensures that no one has a chance to respond to your bid, but it also increases the chances of something going wrong and your bid not being placed. It is up to each user to select what they consider to be the best compromise time.

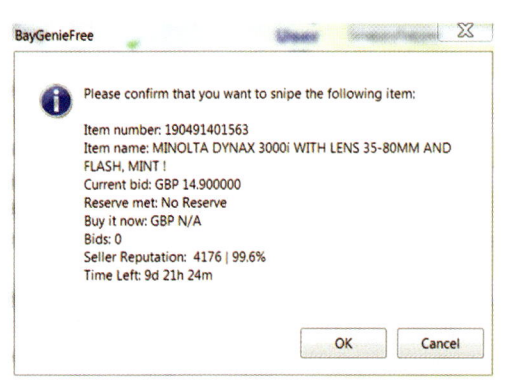

Fig.1.11   Operate the OK button if all the details are correct

With all the information entered it is then just a matter of operating the Snipe It button, and you will

EBay buying 1

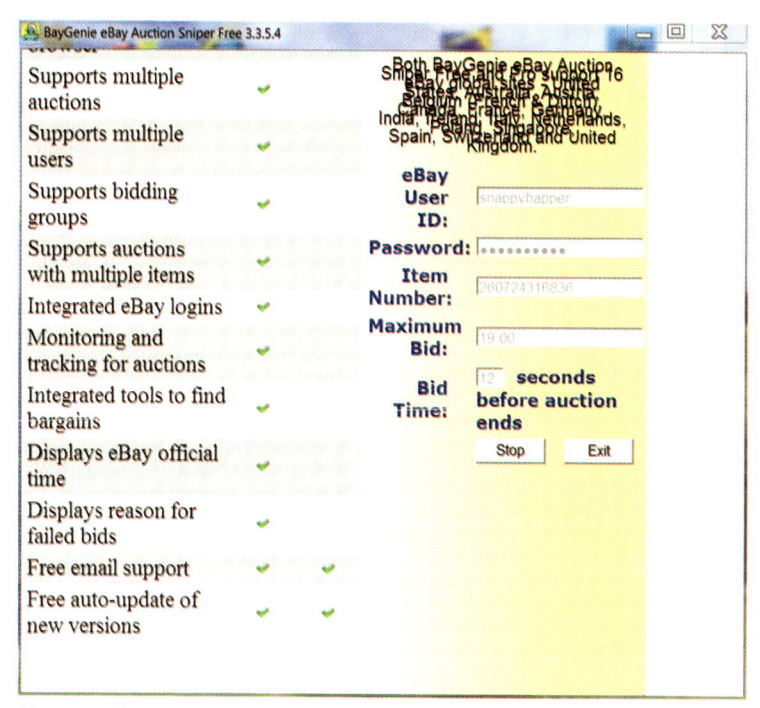

Fig.1.12 Use the Stop button if you wish to prevent a bid from being placed

then be asked to confirm the information that you have entered into the program (Figure 1.11). If you operate the OK button, in due course the program will try to place your bid. Of course, if the bidding exceeds your maximum bid price before it is time for your bid to be placed, no bid can be made by the program. You can change your mind and prevent a bid from being placed by using the Stop button (Figure 1.12), and it is then possible to set up the program to snipe on another item. The program can be halted by operating the Exit button, but remember that a bid can only be placed by the program if it is still "up and running" just before the end of the auction is reached. All the information entered into the program is lost when exiting it. Entering the appropriate information into the program, closing it, and then starting the program again as the end of the auction approaches will not work. The correct way to use the program is to set it up correctly when the end of the auction is getting close, and then leave it running until the auction has ended.

17

1   EBay buying

Fig.1.13 The program can be used for a 15 day trial period

Pro version

The Pro version of BayGenie is a much more sophisticated piece of software that has a wide range of features. The screen of Figure 1.13 is obtained the first time the program is run, and here you have the choice of registering the program for the appropriate fee or using it free of charge for a 15 day trial period. With anything like this it is always a good idea to take advantage of the free trial period so that you can ensure that it does everything you require before parting with any money.

Operating the Continue Trial button moves things on to the window of Figure 1.14 where your eBay user ID and password are entered. As always with this type of software, both are needed to enable the program to place automatic bids. The checkboxes give the options of having the program remember your password, or sign you in automatically each time the program is run. Both options represent security risks, and it is advisable not to opt for anything of this type when using a portable

EBay buying 1

computer that is easily stolen. Having entered the required information, operating the OK button launches the main program (Figure 1.15).

The program window is divided into two sections with the main program running in the upper section with the lower section providing a web browser. The latter will default to your My eBay page, but it is possible to navigate

Fig.1.14 Enter your eBay ID and password

Fig.1.15 The program has an integrated web browser

1   EBay buying

Fig.1.16 Adding an item to the BayGenie watch list

around the eBay site using the links, menus and search facilities. In use the web browser is used to find an item of interest. The program defaults to the United States version of eBay, so it will usually be necessary to select the appropriate country from the menu near the bottom right-hand corner of the main program, and to then operate the Go button just to the right in order to make your selection the active eBay site. Having found an item of interest, its eBay item number is copied and pasted into the textbox to the left of the countries menu. Operating the Add Watch button then adds the item into the watch list in the upper section of the main program window (Figure 1.16), but before an item is added you must confirm that it is the right one (Figure 1.17).

At this stage it has simply been added to the watch list, and it has to be added to the bidding list if you wish to snipe the item. In order to set up a snipe bid on the item you must left-click on its entry in the watch list to select it, and then operate the Place Bid button in the BayGenie toolbar. By default this will be the third button from the left. Alternatively, you can right-click on the item's entry in the watch list, and then select the Place Bid option from the pop-up menu. Either way, a pop-up window like the one in Figure 1.18 will appear. Make sure that it is for the item you wish

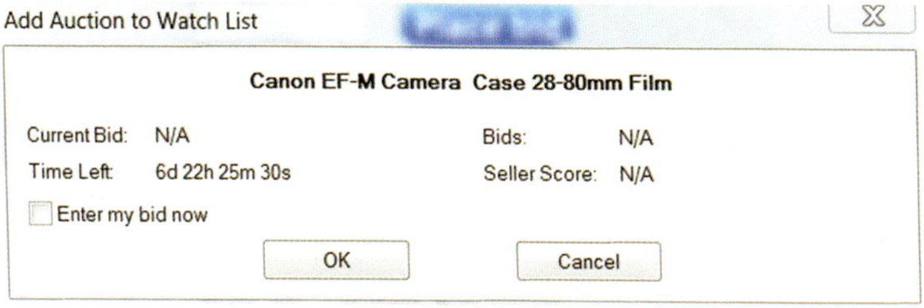

EBay buying 1

Fig.1.17 You must confirm that it is the right item before it is added to the list

to bid on, and then add your bid price to the Maximum Bid textbox. It is advisable to check that the currency is correct, and it should be "GBP" (Great British Pounds) for UK auctions. Where appropriate, you can enter the number of items you wish to buy.

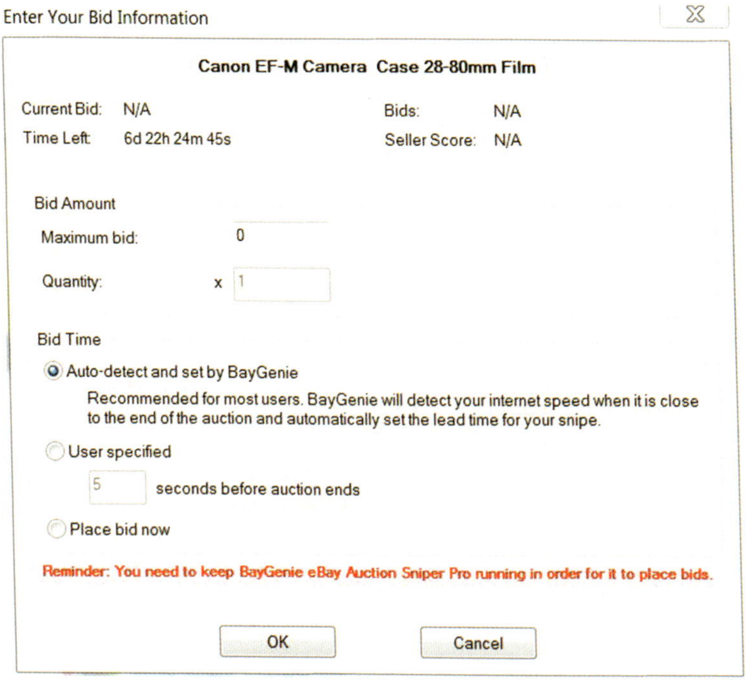

Fig.1.18 This window is used to set up a sniping bid

21

1   EBay buying

Fig.1.19   The item has now been added to the BayGenie bidding list

In the lower section of the window there are three radio buttons. The top and middle buttons respectively provide the options of having the program detect the speed of connection and place the bid at the appropriate time, or having the bid placed at a preset number of seconds before the end of the auction. The automatic option will usually suffice, but a time can be set manually if you prefer to "play safe" and have the bid placed (say) 20 or 30 seconds before the auction closes. The third radio button enables the bid to be placed immediately.

Operate the OK button when the required information has been added and the appropriate options have been selected. Details of the newly entered snipe will then appear in the BayGenie bidding list (Figure 1.19). Remember that the bid can only be placed if you have signed into BayGenie and it is running when it is time for the bid to be placed. Obviously it is also necessary for the computer to have an active Internet connection that is working properly so that BayGenie can contact the eBay site and place the bid. Any form of sniping from your own PC is unlikely to be very successful if your Internet connection is of the "hit and miss" variety. Using a sniping site is likely to be a better approach

EBay buying 1

Fig.1.20 Bids can be cancelled using the pop-up menu

unless your Internet connection is something close to one hundred percent reliable.

Keeping track

The left-hand section of the main program window makes it easy to keep track of the items you are bidding on, or have already bid on. Of course, essentially the same facilities are available from your My eBay page, but you must go to the BayGenie program to obtain details of sniping bids that have not yet been placed. Also, if the bidding exceeds your maximum price before your bid is placed, BayGenie will not be able to place a bid. With no bid placed, the item will not appear in any section of your My eBay page, other than the watch list if you decide to include it here as well as in the BayGenie program. For details of failed bids you must look in the Didn't Win section of the BayGenie program.

If you change your mind and wish to cancel a bid, select the Bidding section in the left-hand panel of the main program window, and then right-click the appropriate entry in the main panel. This produces a pop-up menu (Figure 1.20) where the Cancel Bids option is selected. You will be asked to confirm the deletion, and the bid will be removed from the Bidding list if the OK button is operated. It is worth noting that multiple items can be deleted by using the normal Windows methods for making a multiple selection, and then right-clicking on one of the selected items to produce the pop-up menu. The process is then the same as for a single deletion.

You will probably wish to have items in BayGenie also included in the Watch List of your My eBay page, and vice versa. BayGenie has an

1 **EBay buying**

Fig.1.21 Four types of list can be imported from eBay

import facility that makes it easy to keep the two watch lists synchronised, and this probably represents the easiest way of entering items into the BayGenie program. First populate the eBay watch list in the normal way, and then run BayGenie. In the BayGenie program, choose the Import Items From My eBay from the Action menu. A small window like the one in Figure 1.21 will then pop up, and this enables four categories from your My eBay page to be imported into BayGenie's lists.

Remove the ticks from the checkboxes for any lists that you do not wish to import. This will usually mean removing all the ticks apart from the one in the top checkbox. For this example I opted to import the four items in the watch list, but nothing else. When the required selection has been made, operate the Import button. The appropriate items will then be added to the BayGenie Watch List, but this could take a minute or two if a large number of items are involved. The pop-up window will show how things are progressing, and eventually the process will be finished (Figure 1.22).

Fig.1.22 It might take a while, but the import process will eventually be completed

24

EBay buying   1

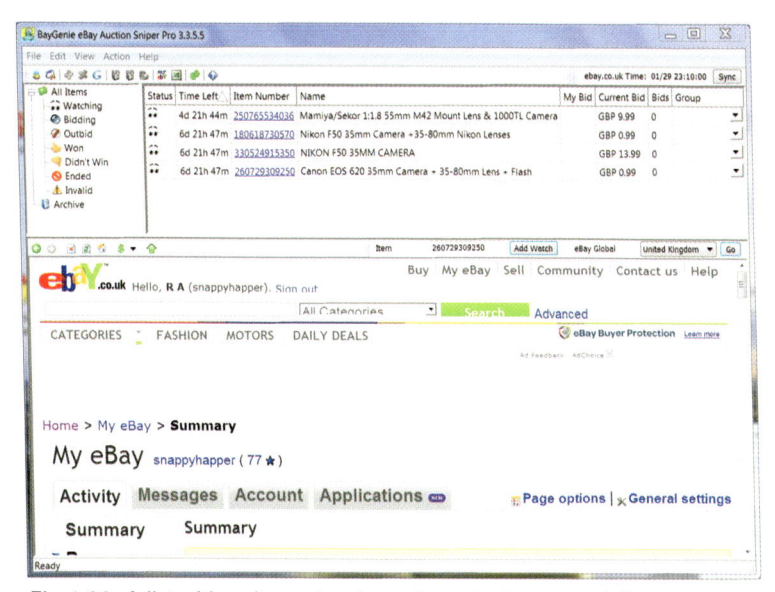

Fig.1.23 A list of four items has been imported successfully

Operate the Exit button to close the window and then check that the items have been imported into BayGenie. In this case everything worked correctly, and the four items were imported into BayGenie (Figure 1.23).

Group bidding

BayGenie is a highly specified program, and amongst other things it can support multiple users. It also supports bidding groups, which is used when you need to place bids on a string of auctions, automatically stopping when one of them has been won. For example, I often place bids on auctions for a particular make and model of camera, but stop as soon as I win an auction because I only want one of that particular camera.

This can be achieved by entering the snipes into the program one by one until an auction is won, but this is not very convenient if several of the auctions come along in rapid succession. Buying opportunities could easily be missed. Another way is to enter several snipes, and to delete any that remain once the required item has been purchased. The obvious snag here is that you might not cancel the unwanted items in time, and

25

1   EBay buying

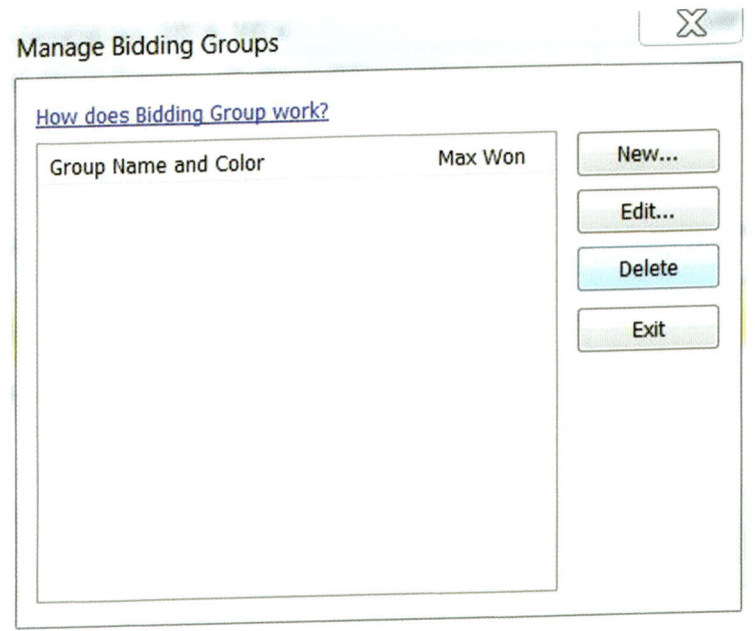

Fig.1.24 The window used to manage groups

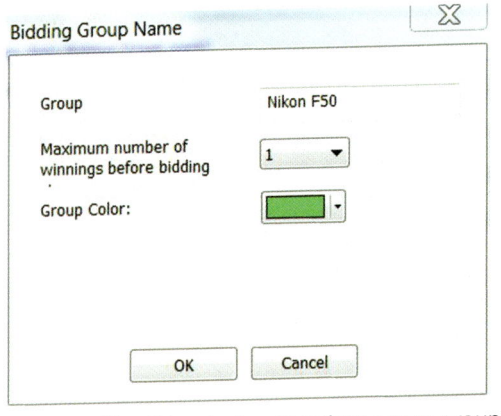

Fig. 1.25 Use this window to set up a new group

could end up buying two or three of them! In fact this is quite likely to happen if several of the auctions end within a few minutes of each other. With BayGenie's automated group bidding system there is no risk of missing opportunities or buying too many of the item even if several auctions end within the space of a few minutes.

With the Groups feature of BayGenie you must first create a new group. The first step is to choose the Manage Groups

EBay buying 1

option from the Action menu, and the small pop-up window of Figure 1.24 will then appear. The main panel on the left lists the existing groups, but at this stage there will obviously be no groups to list. A group is added to the list by operating the New button to produce the new pop-up window of Figure 1.25, and setting the required parameters. The name for the group should be something apposite, and in this case I am bidding on Nikon F50 cameras, so I have called the group "Nikon F50".

The pop-down menu in the middle controls the number of items that are won before the bidding process is halted. This is useful if you wish to buy several items of the same type, but in most cases only one example of the item will be required and the default value will suffice. The pop-down menu at the bottom is used to select the colour for the group, and this is simply the background colour that will be used for the items entries in the various BayGenie lists. Provided you use a totally different colour for each group, this enables you to see at a glance which items are in a particular group.

Operate the OK button when the required settings have been entered. This closes the window, and the new group should then be listed

Fig.1.26 The new group has be created

in the Manage Bidding Groups window (Figure 1.26). Operate the Exit button to close this window, and you can then start adding items from the Watching list to the new group. This is done by double-clicking the group field for an entry in the list, and selecting the required group from the drop-down menu (Figure 1.27). In this example there is only one group to choose from, but if you add more groups they will be included in this menu. Repeat the selection process for all the items you wish to include in the group. I included six items in the group (Figure 1.28), which are shown with the appropriate background colour in the Watching list. It is then just a matter of setting up a bid on each item in the usual way.

1 EBay buying

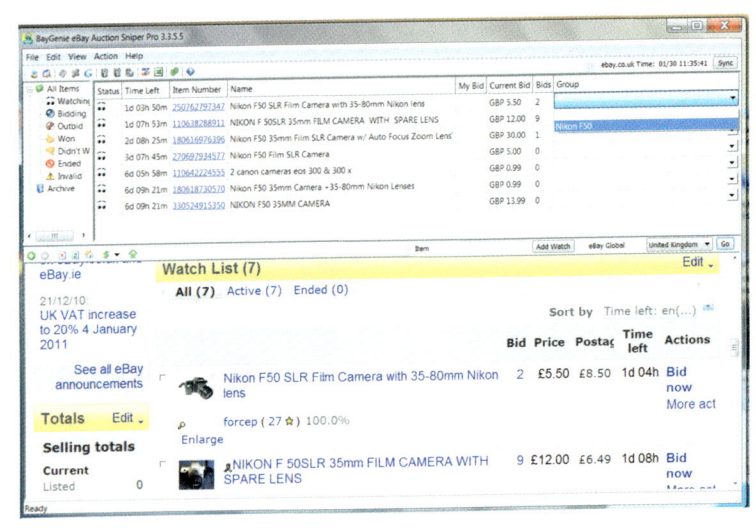

Fig.1.27 Adding a watching list item to a group

Online bidding sites

No matter how sophisticated a sniping program might be, it always has a major drawback. Unless your computer is running, has an active Internet connection, and the bidding program is also running, a bid cannot be placed. In cases where the Internet connection is a bit iffy, the bidding will probably be unreliable unless bids are placed well ahead of the auction's closing times. Proper sniping is not possible unless you are prepared to accept a few failures due to bids not being placed in time. The same problem exists if sniping bids are placed manually using a slow or unreliable Internet connection.

Web sites that place sniping bids for you provide a way around these problems. These sites operate 24 hours a day, and will place bids at any time of the day or night. They have fast Internet connections that give good reliability, and the quality of the user's Internet connection is not important. Provided you can actually get online and access the web site to set up your bids, everything should go according to plan.

On the downside, in order to use any facility of this type you have to supply your eBay user ID and password to the company that provides the service. This is, of course, something that you are always advised not to do, and it is something that should definitely not be done unless

EBay buying 1

Fig.1.28 The items in green have been added to the "F50" group

you are sure that the company concerned can be trusted. Another problem with these services is that apart from any free initial trial period, they mostly require a subscription to be paid. In most cases the subscriptions are not very high, but over a period of time they can mount up. Of course, this is also true of most auction sniping programs, and I suppose that the paid-for software and services are only likely to be worthwhile if you are a professional user or a dedicated amateur user of eBay.

Anyway, a free online auction service is available from www.goofbay.com, or www.goofbay.co.uk. This site has other facilities, but here we will only consider its online auction sniping feature. There is no charge for using the online sniping service; although you can make a donation to the site should you wish to do so. It is an established site that has a good reputation, and I have used it without experiencing any problems. Whether you trust any site with your eBay user ID and password is something you have to decide for yourself though.

Using Goofbay

A number of facilities are available from the Feature Tools section of the Goofbay homepage (Figure 1.29), but here it is the Free eBay Sniper tool in the top left-hand corner that is of interest. The item number is

29

1 EBay buying

Fig.1.29 The Goofbay homepage

copied from the listing and pasted into the textbox. Operating the button next to the textbox then moves things on to the next stage (Figure 1.30), where you sign into Goofbay. If you are new to Goofbay it will be

Fig.1.30 You must sign in to Goofbay to use the sniping facility

EBay buying 1

Fig.1.31 Use this page to enter details of the sniping bid

necessary to go through a simple registration process before proceeding further. There is a link near the bottom of the page that gives access to the registration page.

Once signed in you are taken to the page where details of the sniping bid are entered (Figure 1.31). There is a link near the middle of the page that can be used to check that the item number you have entered is for the right item. Using this link opens the selected listing page in a new tab or window, depending on the way that your web browser is set up. In this example the listing appeared in a new window (Figure 1.32). Operate the Confirm Item button when you are sure that the correct item number has been used. Your eBay user ID and password are then entered into the two textboxes. It is your eBay user ID and password that are entered here, and not your Goofbay sign-in details, which should be different to the ones used for eBay.

Your maximum bid price is entered in the Maximum Bid textbox, and the currency in use will be shown here. In this case a pound sign is displayed, and the currency in use is British pounds. By default your bid will be placed when there are five seconds left for the auction to run, but the drop-down menu near the bottom of the page enables a longer time to be selected if desired. Operate the Add Snipe button when all the necessary information has been added and checked. This moves things

31

1 EBay buying

Fig.1.32 You can check that the right listing has been selected

on to a page that shows details of your forthcoming bid (Figure 1.33), and in due course the bid will be placed for you by the Goofbay system.

You are not limited to one snipe at a time with Goofbay, and more sniping bids can be added if desired. The Remove Snipe link can be used if you

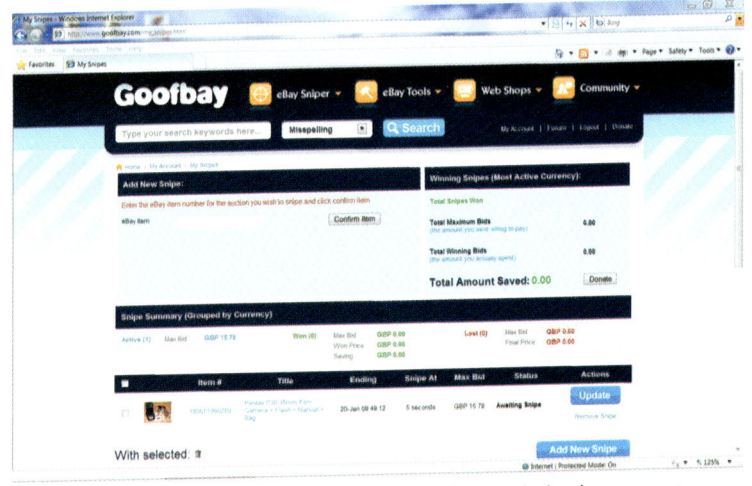

Fig.1.33 The bid has been set up and will be made in due course

EBay buying 1

Fig.1.34 If necessary, a bid can be edited

Fig.1.35 Select the My Account link near the top right-hand corner

33

1   EBay buying

Fig.1.36 This page has links to pages that control various aspects of the account

change your mind and would like to cancel a forthcoming bid. Use the Update button should you need to amend a bid. This changes the window to one that is essentially the same as the one used to set up the original bid (Figure 1.34), and it is just a matter of making the required change or changes and then operating the Update Snipe button.

From time to time it will be necessary to return to the page that lists your snipes, and this is achieved by first going to the Goofbay homepage and signing in using the Login link near the top right-hand corner of the page. After logging in you are taken to a page that looks rather like the homepage (Figure 1.35), but the links near the top right-hand corner of the page are slightly different. Use the My Account link to go to the page shown in Figure 1.36, where there are links to pages that control various aspects of your Goofbay account. The My Snipes button takes you to the page where your snipes can be monitored and edited (Figure 1.37).

EBay buying 1

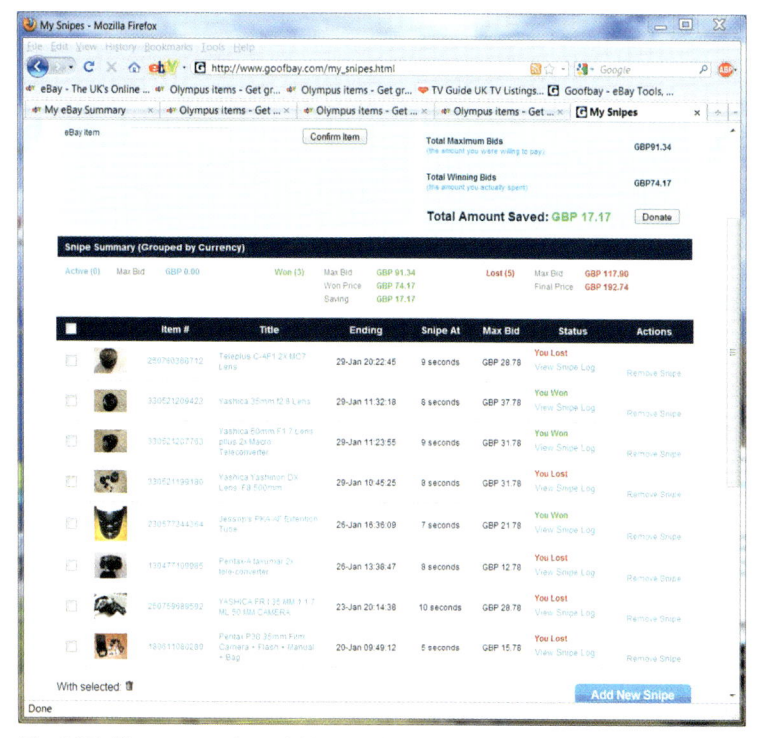

Fig.1.37 The page where bids can be monitored, added, and edited

Sniping Button

Goofbay provide an alternative way of using their sniping service, which is to use a button added to the Favourites or Bookmarks bar of your web browser. Goofbay call this facility their Bookmarklet. I found that this worked well with the Mozilla Firefox browser, but I could not get it to work at all with Internet Explorer. Installing the button is very easy, and the first step is to go to the page that gives details of your snipes. Near the bottom of this page there is the section shown in Figure 1.38, which includes the blue Goofbay-Add Snipe button. If the Bookmarks toolbar is not already active, go to the View menu, choose the Toolbars option, and then select Bookmarks Toolbar from the drop-down submenu. It is then just a matter of dragging the Goofbay-Add Snipe button from the page to an empty section of the Bookmarks toolbar, and the new button is then ready for use (Figure 1.39).

35

1 EBay buying

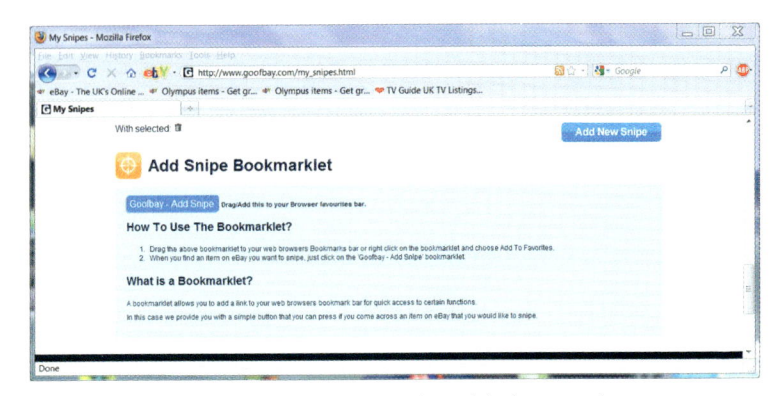

Fig.1.38 A Goofbay snipe button can be added to your browser

In order to use the button it is a matter of first going to the listing page for the item you wish to bid on. Operating the button should then produce a small pop-up window (Figure 1.40), but it will be preceded by a miniature version of the Goofbay login page if you are not already logged into the site. Having reached the window of Figure 1.40, in the normal way you should first check that the item number is correct. Also as normal, you must confirm that the item number is correct, and add your maximum bid price to the textbox. If necessary, the Snipe At time can be altered using the drop-down menu.

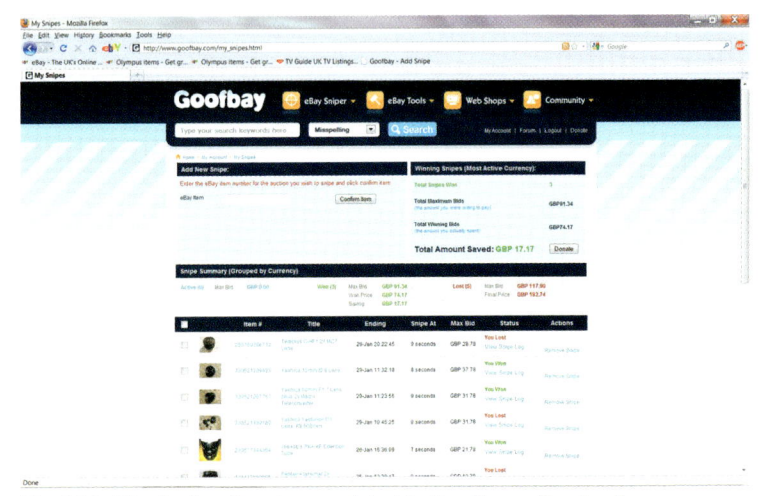

Fig.1.39 The button has been added to the Favourites toolbar

EBay buying 1

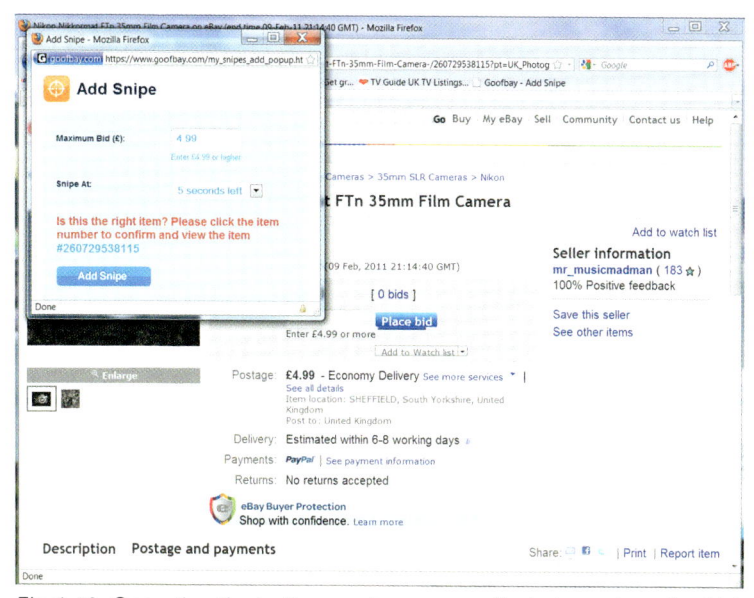

Fig.1.40 Operating the button produces a small window where the bid price is entered

Operate the Add Snipe button when everything is as it should be, and the bid will be added to your list of snipes. Provided everything works as it should, the small pop-up window of Figure 1.41 will confirm that the snipe has been added successfully. Initially it is probably as well to go to the page that lists your snipes and check that the new one has been added to the list. In this case

Fig.1.41 The new snipe has been added

37

1   EBay buying

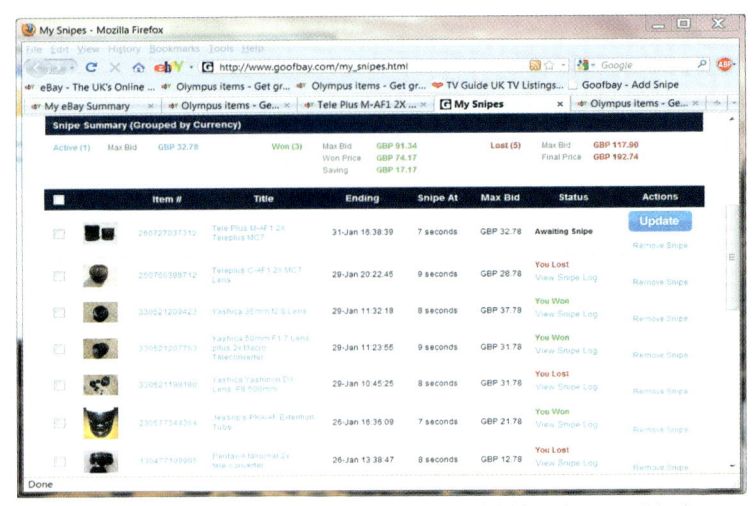

Fig.1.42 The snipe list confirms that the new bid has been added

it was added to the list (Figure 1.42) and the bid was placed in due course.

The Goofbay sniping facility is not as sophisticated as some of the paid-for online sniping sites and software, but it has sufficient facilities to satisfy most amateur users. In my experience it works well, and not having to be online when the bid is placed gives it a massive advantage over sniping software running on your own computer. You just enter details of your snipe and then have to do nothing else apart from checking later to see if you won. As free online services go, it seems to be one of the best.

Shill bidding

Sniping guards against a process known as "shill bidding", or "artificial bidding" as it is also known. This is where the seller uses a second eBay account, or the account of a friend, to place bids on their own auctions. In some cases the idea is to push the bidding up to the price bid by the current highest bidder. One way this is done is to place a high shill bid on the item in order to determine the bid price placed by the victim, and then the bid is retracted. A little later on a shill bid using a different account is placed just below the victim's maximum bid, taking the current bid price up to that level. More usually, the shill bidding is in the form of numerous bids, with each one moving the price a little higher in an attempt to find the victim's maximum bid price without actually exceeding it.

Sniping is not popular with sellers because, in general, it holds down prices. Also, a seller likes to see steady bidding with the price gradually moving up towards the price they would like to obtain. It is a strain on the nerves if you are selling an item worth about five hundred pounds and the bid price is two pounds and fifty pence with the auction due to close in ten seconds time! However, it is up to buyers to look after their own interests and not those of the seller. Sniping helps to reduce the price paid for eBay items and also reduces the chances of you becoming a victim of shill bidding. It is a legitimate tactic and it makes sense to use it.

Use PayPal

You might occasionally buy something from someone living close enough for collection in person and payment by cash to be a practical proposition, but most purchases on eBay fall into the "distance selling" category. In other words, you use a method of payment other than cash, and the goods are delivered by the Royal Mail or a courier service. With any form of distance selling there is a risk of the money being paid but no goods being received. With distance selling and buying via eBay the risks can be minimised by using PayPal to pay for purchases. There are additional costs with PayPal transfers, but these are borne by the seller, as are all the eBay fees. Buying items on eBay and using PayPal to pay for them is totally free from fees and surcharges.

PayPal used to be totally separate from eBay, but the company was bought by eBay some years ago and has to some extent been integrated with the eBay system. You must open a PayPal account in order to make use of this method of sending and receiving money, and your PayPal account can be linked to credit and debit cards and to a bank account. Once you have set up the account it is easy to pay for eBay items that have this payment option. Since it is compulsory for this payment method to be offered when selling most types of goods, it will nearly always be available as a means of payment. You can use PayPal by going through the eBay checkout system, and instant payments can be made from the cards or bank account linked to the PayPal account.

It is a good idea to pay in this way for two main reasons, one of which is simply that it is an instant transfer system, and it avoids having to wait while cheque payments are cleared. There is a version of PayPal payment called an "E-cheque", but it is best to avoid this as far as possible as it is far from instant, and it usually takes about 10-14 days for the payment to clear. The second, and perhaps more important reason for using PayPal,

1 EBay buying

is that you can make a claim from PayPal if the goods are not received, or are significantly different to the description in the listing. This greatly reduces the risk of buying items via eBay. Note that you must use one of the PayNow buttons and go through the eBay/PayPal payment system in order to get this security. Do not pay for eBay items by going through the normal PayPal system for making general payments for goods and services.

Nearly new bargains?

I would guess that most people buying on eBay are looking for bargains, and are trying to obtain goods well below their normal market value. At the most simple level, people are simply looking for second-hand goods at something well below the price of a new equivalent. There are sometimes quite dramatic price differences between nearly new second-hand items and the same thing obtained brand new. There are a couple of points to bear in mind though, and one of these is that the recommended retail prices set by manufacturers are often much higher than a typical shop price. The price from on-line discount sellers can be even lower.

Where appropriate, always check the actual selling prices of new goods before trying to buy them second-hand on eBay or elsewhere. With popular items the differences can be surprisingly small, and you might even find second-hand goods on eBay selling for more than the lowest price for new goods! The difference otherwise tends to be quite high, with a saving of around fifty percent when buying second-hand. The second important point to keep in mind is that second-hand goods do not come complete with a statutory guarantee. The vendor might give some sort of guarantee on the goods, but in most cases they are sold without any form of warranty. You are then taking a chance and gambling that the goods will go on working properly for a reasonable period. It now seems to be the norm for the cost of repairing goods to be higher than their second-hand value, so items that become faulty are often valueless. It is probably not worthwhile buying second-hand unless you can obtain the item at a really good discount to the cost of a new one.

Second chance offers

The eBay system includes a facility whereby a seller can offer items to non-winning bidders. The item offered must either be the one in the listing, or an identical item. Note that you will only receive second chance offers if the appropriate option is selected in your account settings. There can be legitimate reasons for a seller making one or more second chance offers. The most likely reason is that the winning bidder has contacted the seller and made it clear that they will not be completing the sale. If you receive a second chance offer long after the auction ended, it is likely that the winning bidder has not contacted the seller and that the seller has cancelled the sale. Where a seller has several identical items for sale they might list and sell one item, and then offer one or more of the other items to losing bidders who have bid reasonably high amounts. While this might give lower selling prices than auctioning the other items in the normal way, it is relatively quick and easy for the seller, and it also avoids paying additional listing fees. The seller still has to pay the final value fee on second chance offers incidentally.

You need to be a little cautious when receiving second chance offers. There have been various scams in the past that were based on second chance offers. In the main these were based on bogus offers that did not come from the original seller. Changes to the eBay system have to a large extent foiled these scams, but you still have to make sure that any second chance offers are received through the eBay messaging system and not only via the email account that you use in conjunction with eBay. Another scam combines second chance offers with shill bidding. The seller places a very high bid on his or her own item, thus ensuring that this is the winning bid. A second chance offer is then made to the bidder with the highest legitimate bid. The point of this is to ensure that the item sells for the highest possible price. It is usually difficult to determine with any certainty whether the winning bid was a legitimate one or a shill bid, and I suppose you might be quite happy to buy the item at your maximum bid price anyway. On the other hand, many buyers prefer to "play safe" and have nothing to do with second chance offers. You have to come to your own decision on this one, but initially at any rate, it is probably best not to take up any second chance offers.

Risky bargains

Many people put a great deal of effort into obtaining real bargains on eBay, and try to obtain goods at a fraction of their normal market value. This can be done, but it is probably much easier for those with a great deal of experience at buying on eBay. Trying to buy the best bargains on eBay is also a bit more risky, and you could end up buying a load of rubbish with little chance of getting your money back. By taking risks that most others are not prepared to take it is possible to obtain massive bargains, but you are likely to waste a certain amount of money as well.

1 EBay buying

You should end up "well ahead of the game" provided you get things right in the majority of cases.

As a seller, you should get good prices if you put in the effort and list things well. Conversely, you tend to get low prices, and in some cases spectacularly so, if you do not put in the effort and make a mess of things. From the bargain hunter's point of view, it therefore follows that very professionally listed items are unlikely to be a good source of goods at below par prices. In fact the more inept the listing, the better your chances of obtaining a real bargain! The risk is that a listing could be deliberately inept in order to cover up some shortcomings in the item for sale. There might be a possibility of getting a refund through PayPal if the seller is uncooperative and that was the method of payment used. However, it can be difficult to claim that goods were "substantially not as described" if the description is so vague as to be largely meaningless! These are some types of listing to try if you are going to seek out the mega-bargains, and you are prepared to take a risk.

No photograph

Many buyers on eBay will not buy a second-hand item unless there are some reasonable photographs of the item so that they can see what they are buying, and they are in a good position to assess its condition. In particular, those prepared to bid high prices are unlikely to bid on an item unless they can see that it is in good condition. This will often leave you to battle it out with the other bargain hunters

Terrible photograph

Once again, many potential bidders will have nothing to do with items where they cannot see what they are buying. If you are prepared to take the risk you might get a bargain, but in my experience this is a little riskier than buying items where there are no photographs at all. Sometimes there are one or two general photographs that are quite good, but the close-up shots are very blurred. With small items this is usually the result of the photographer getting the camera too close to the subject, rendering the camera unable to focus properly. Be very suspicious if all the photographs are blurred. Also be very suspicious if they are photographed in a very inept way, such as the item on offer being so small in the photograph that you can barely see it, or a case being carefully positioned so that it largely obliterates your view of the item that goes in it.

EBay buying 1

Fig.1.43 This grossly underexposed photograph shows little detail

Photo processing

When a listing includes poor quality photographs it is sometimes possible to process them so that you can see more detail. This will not always be possible, and there is not much that can be done with photographs that are very blurred, only show you the top half of the item for sale, or something of this nature. You can try to adjust an overexposed photograph using a photo-editing program, but it is not usually possible to rescue any worthwhile detail from burned-out highlights. The situation is very different with underexposed photographs, where it is often possible to lift a surprising amount of detail from virtually black areas of the picture. Figure 1.43 shows a photograph that is underexposed by at least two stops, but there is still a reasonable amount of detail in the processed version of Figure 1.44.

Practically any photo-editing software should have facilities for adjusting the exposure and lightening shadow areas. One slight problem is that the normal Copy and Paste or Save As functions might not work properly

1 EBay buying

Fig.1.44 The edited image shows a great deal more detail

when applied to eBay images. An easy way around the problem is to display the large version of a photograph and then operate the Print Screen key to copy the screen to the clipboard. This image can then be pasted onto a blank page in the image editor, where the unwanted parts of the screen can be cropped. The image can then be processed in the normal way.

Reserve price

On the face of it, bidding should be the same whether or not an item has a reserve price. In reality it does not seem to work this way, and reserve prices often seem to act as a deterrent to bidders. Presumably many potential bidders assume that the reserve price is high and that it is therefore not worth bidding on the item. Anyway, the reserve price might not be particularly high, and you might win if you place a reasonable bid. It is sometimes possible to obtain a bargain with a very modest bid if that bid is the highest one but is still below the reserve price. The seller might decide that your winning bid price is about as much as they are likely to get for the item, and rather than relist it they might send you a second chance offer. It is best to decline if they contact you and try to sell you the item at a figure beyond the winning bid price. Decline any offers to trade outside eBay. Apart from breaking the eBay rules, you obviously lose the normal eBay safeguards if you accept a private deal.

High Buy-it-Now price

High Buy-it-Now prices added to an ordinary auction listing also tend to put people off bidding. Presumably most people see the high Buy-it-Now price and do not bother to investigate any further. If the starting price is quite low it is virtually certain that someone will place a bid before too long. Provided there is no reserve price, the Buy-it-Now option will disappear and the auction will then continue normally. Things are more interesting if the starting price is relatively high, but not unreasonably so. This creates a good chance of the Buy-it-Now staying in place until close to the end of the auction, keeping interest in the item very low. A bid at or just above the starting price might then be successful. The same method can work with any item that has a starting price that is high for a starting price, but would represent a bargain as the final price. It works better when there is also an inflated Buy-it-Now price to deter would-be bidders, but a high starting price on its own is sometimes sufficient to hold down the final price.

Low feedback

A seller can have a low feedback score simply because they managed to get into a dispute with one buyer, and they have sold few items in the last few months. If they have an exemplary feedback record in other respects they are probably good sellers and a reasonably safe bet. The low feedback score will prevent many people from bidding on their items, which makes them likely candidates for bargains. Even lower prices can be obtained by bidding on items from sellers who have genuinely terrible feedback records, but it is probably best not to do so.

Wrong category

A surprising number of items are listed in an inappropriate category. Sometimes it is due to sellers listing an item in two categories. This is encouraged by eBay as it can help sellers to get higher selling prices, and it also increases the fees earned by eBay. The problem is that with many items there is no second category that is really suitable. The secondary listing is unlikely to increase the final selling price, but it is unlikely to decrease it either. It is when an item is only listed in one or more inappropriate categories that things become more interesting.

This can occur when the seller is lacking in knowledge about the item they are selling, or get careless when listing an item. The eBay system suggests categories when you list an item, and it usually does quite a good job. However, it will usually list some inappropriate categories along with one or two wholly relevant ones. Anyone opting to simply take the first one or two suggestions on the list could easily end up placing the item in categories where it will be seen by few prospective buyers. The lesson here for buyers is to not narrow eBay searches to one or two categories. Searching an entire section of eBay (photography, consumer electronics, etc.) might produce the occasional bargain that would otherwise be missed.

Buying from abroad

When you are new to eBay it is probably best to only buy items from people and companies based in your home country. Buying items from abroad is mostly straightforward, but it is advisable to gain some experience at buying on eBay before taking on the small additional risk of dealing with sellers based in other countries. If you do eventually start buying from abroad it is essential to bear in mind that there can be expenses other than the usual cost of the item itself and any postage and packing charges.

In order to obtain the usual eBay buyer protection it is advisable to pay for items brought from abroad using PayPal, and it is likely that this will be the only practical method anyway. There is no charge as such for paying in a currency other than the one of your home country, but as is often the case with this type of thing, the exchange rate used might not be the best on offer. In effect, a small charge might effectively be levied via the exchange rate. This can result in the price of the item and any delivery charge being a little higher than expected, but only a little.

In the UK there are no customs duties to pay when importing items that cost less than 18 pounds, so there should be no additional expenses when buying items that cost less than this threshold value. Items that exceed the threshold value will be liable to value added tax, and possibly other duties and handling charges. These are of far more significance than any increase in the price due to an unfavourable exchange rate, and could easily boost the total price paid by 25 to 30 percent. When bidding you must therefore deduct about 25 percent from the maximum price you are prepared to pay in order to allow for these additional charges, or you might end up paying far more than you originally intended to.

Another point to bear in mind is that it can be expensive if you need to return goods to another country. It can be expensive if you have to pay the return postage, and very expensive if you end up paying the postage and packing costs in both directions. It is unlikely that you will be able to get any import duties and charges repaid, but if the return paperwork is completed properly it should not be necessary for the seller to pay any duties when the goods are returned to them. After receiving a refund you are likely to still be substantially out of pocket.

Understand the description

Items listed on the UK eBay site should have the product descriptions in English even if they are being sold from another country. Admittedly some of the descriptions are in something approximating to English rather than being written in the genuine article. Even so, you can usually ascertain that the item is actually the one you require. If not, it is probably best to resist the temptation to buy it.

The situation is trickier if you start buying items from eBay sites for other countries where the descriptions are in a language that you do not understand. I once met a fellow camera enthusiast who had bought a camera from the German eBay site at what seemed to be a bargain price.

He was not suspicious of the very low selling price as the camera was one that was manufactured in what at the time was East Germany. It was therefore in relatively plentiful supply in the reunited Germany, and tended to cost less than in the UK. However, it had a couple of serious faults, and on getting the product description translated he discovered that these were described in some detail. He was therefore unable to return the item, and the cost of getting it repaired was about four times the initial cost of purchasing the camera!

Translation

The obvious mistake he made was to get the description of the camera translated into English after he bought it instead of before he placed a bid. There are numerous translation services available on the Internet. Many of these are free, but all the free translation services I have

1 EBay buying

Fig.1.45 The text to be translated is pasted into the textbox

encountered are performed using software rather than a human translator. The quality of the translations from these varies somewhat, and to some extent it will depend on the excellence of the source. A translation is unlikely to be perfectly clear if the original description is poorly written.

Anyway, if you cannot translate the description yourself, and you do not know anyone who can do it for you, it is advisable to use some form of translation service. With an expensive item it might be worthwhile paying to have it translated by a linguist, but in most cases an automatic translation from a free online service will have to suffice. While the resultant prose might not be perfect, the translated description should be adequate to provide some warning signs if the description includes details of any faults. Any problems with items are often highlighted in the description by (say) having them in bright red lettering, so that buyers cannot reasonably claim that they did not notice the relevant section and thought that they were buying perfect goods. Pay particular attention to any parts of the description that have been designed to stand out. The seller might be emphasising the strong points of the item, but it is more likely that deficiencies are being highlighted.

Fig.1.46 The translated text has the required information

Goods sold on eBay used to be categorised simply as "new" or "used", but there are now additional categories for most items. One of these new categories is for goods that are "For parts or not working". Unless you actually need an item for spare parts or to repair, anything in this category should obviously be avoided. Unfortunately, it is not safe to assume that an item listed as "used" will be fully working. Where something has a minor fault but is still fully usable it is unlikely to be listed as "For parts or not working". For instance, a film camera that has a faulty frame counter but is otherwise working is still fully usable. Unless you keep count yourself you will not know how many pictures you have taken. This is an inconvenience, but the camera will still take perfectly good photographs.

An item of this type is likely to be listed as "used" rather than "For parts or not working". With "used" items it is still important to understand the item descriptions. Finding a suitable free translation service should be very easy provided neither of the languages involved is out of the ordinary. It is just a matter of using "free", "translation" and the two languages as search terms in any good search engine. For this example I used the description of a camera that was listed on the German eBay site, and I had it translated by www.freetranslation.com simply because this was the first site in the list of results from the search engine.

The text is copied from the listing and pasted into the left-hand textbox on the translation page using the Copy and Paste facilities of the web browser. The next step with this type of thing is to choose the source and destination languages from drop-down menus, but in this case the auto-detection system correctly identified the source as being in German. Accordingly, I only had to choose the destination language and operate the Translate button in order to obtain the translated text in the right-hand textbox. Figure 1.46 shows the final part of the translation, and although this is in slightly "broken" English, it does make it clear that in this case the item is being sold as in fully working condition.

2

Selling on eBay

eBay selling

Good marketing is all-important when trying to sell practically anything. This is true whether a car company is trying to sell half million pound cars or an individual is trying to sell off some second-hand possessions that are no longer needed. In either case, marketing the goods in an inept fashion will either result in no sales or the items for sale "going for a song". In order to sell goods at good prices it is necessary to go about things the right way.

This is certainly the case when selling your surplus items on eBay. Virtually identical items often sell on eBay at widely differing prices, and I have seen two examples of the same product where one has sold at about ten times the price of the other. The two items were in similar condition, and it was not a case of one being in mint condition and the other being faulty. With auctions there is always a degree of "hit and miss", and two identical items are unlikely to sell at precisely the same price. However, large differences are usually the result of one seller putting in some effort and doing a good job, while the other has not really tried or has simply made a mess of things.

Photographs

Including a photograph of the item for sale is not a requirement of eBay, but few things, if any, will sell well unless the listing features at least one good photograph of the actual item for sale. The first photograph is included in the basic listing fee, but there is a small charge for any further photographs that are used. The eBay system includes stock photographs for a range of popular consumer goods, and they are also available elsewhere. These are mainly intended for those selling new goods, where the item on offer will be as pristine as the one in the photograph. When selling second-hand goods it is not a good idea to use stock pictures of new items. When doing so it is essential to make it clear that the photograph is not a picture of the item on offer. People buying second-

2 Selling on eBay

Fig.2.1 An inexpensive second-hand camera such as this is sufficient for taking pictures to use in eBay listings

hand goods want to know the condition of the item for sale, and a stock photograph tells them no more than having no picture at all.

If you do not already have a digital camera it is worth buying a cheap one for eBay use. Photographs on eBay are normally a few hundred pixels on each dimension, although eBay recommend that they should be uploaded at a minimum of about one thousand pixels on the longest dimension. There is the option of paying extra for "Super-Size" pictures, but they are still displayed at a relatively modest size by standards of modern digital cameras. Practically any digital camera can easily handle normal or "Super-Size" pictures, and there is no need for an expensive type that has very high resolution. Something fairly simple should do the job well enough. Note that it is not necessary to upload images to the eBay site at a specific resolution. The eBay system will reduce the pictures to the correct size if you use a higher resolution. If you use a lower resolution the pictures might not be displayed at the maximum size available, so this is best avoided. Also bear in mind that uploading very large image files could be time consuming. Most Internet connections have an upload speed that is much lower than the download speed.

Camera

As already pointed out, a basic digital camera can be obtained quite cheaply second-hand, and these days the price need not be high even if you opt to buy a new one. A good usable digital camera can be obtained very cheaply second-hand on eBay and from charity shops. Someone recently bet me that I could not obtain a working digital camera for less than five pounds. I eventually obtained a quite sophisticated six megapixel camera for ninety nine pence plus the cost of postage (Figure 2.1)! It came with a USB lead, instruction manual, case, and a low capacity memory card that was adequate for taking small batches of photographs for eBay. The only additional cost, apart from the postage charge, was for a couple of AA batteries.

There are certainly plenty of usable second-hand digital cameras available at around ten pounds plus the cost of postage. However, make sure that the camera comes complete with everything needed in order to use it, or that any extras will be inexpensive, such as ordinary batteries. A cheap camera will probably not be a bargain if you have to buy an expensive custom battery, a charger, a USB lead or card reader, and a memory card before you can use it.

Film camera?

Of course, it is not essential to use a digital camera. It is possible to use a film camera and then either scan the prints or negatives to produce files that can be uploaded to eBay. It does not matter too much these days if you do not have a scanner, because most photo processing companies can supply scanned images on a CD-ROM in addition to the normal prints. The extra cost is not usually very high if the CD-ROM is ordered together with the film processing and prints as part of a package deal. Although the resolution of the images might not be particularly high, it should still be more than adequate for uploading to eBay.

Although it is possible to use a film camera when taking photographs for eBay listings, I would certainly advise against doing things this way. With a digital camera you can see the results almost immediately, and if something is amiss you can try again, learning from your mistakes. There are no costs involved beyond those for wear and tear on the equipment used. Matters are very different if you make a mess of things using a film camera. Trying again is likely to be a relatively slow and expensive business.

Using a film camera will not be very cost-effective even if you manage to get it right first time, every time. The cost of film and processing is quite high in comparison to the cost of a cheap second hand digital camera. Even taking one batch of photographs could cost more than an inexpensive but usable second-hand digital camera. The cost of several batches of photographs taken using a film camera would probably far exceed the cost of a basic but very good digital camera bought new. A digital camera is the more practical option when taking photographs for use on eBay.

Scanning

A flatbed scanner can sometimes be used when producing images for use on eBay. With some items a scanner might be better than a camera, and this is likely to be the case with things like magazines and other publications, CD covers, and anything else that is flat and not too large to fit in your scanner. To some extent it is possible to photograph small 3D objects using most flatbed scanners. As one would probably expect, this way of doing things is a bit limited in scope, and it only works really well with objects that are flattish. The instruction manuals for scanners usually have some advice about scanning 3D objects, and there is plenty of information on this subject available on the Internet.

The subject of photographs for eBay listings will not be considered any further here, but Chapter 3 provides a great deal of advice about taking and processing photographs for your listings. If you are not an expert photographer this should help you to avoid the common mistakes when taking photographs, and to improve images so that they really help to sell your items.

Sections

EBay is divided into various sections and subsections in order to make it easier for buyers to find the type of goods they require. When selling an item it is necessary to specify the section that it will appear in. Some items are appropriate for two sections, and in such cases the same listing can be placed in two sections. For example, a camera lens for a modern digital camera might also fit some film cameras as well, and listing it in both the appropriate sections would increase the chances of obtaining a high selling price. An item cannot be listed in more than two sections, and note that listing in two sections results in all the listing fees being doubled. There is still only one final value fee to pay though.

Heading

Some eBay sellers fail to realise the importance suitable wording in the headings for listings, which tends to be a costly mistake. A heading such as "camera" or "car" is unlikely to bring in dozens of bidders. Most people on seeing a heading such as this will not bother to investigate further. Those that do bother to look at the listing will probably be professional eBay users or experienced amateur users looking to buy things at a fraction of their true value. Most of your potential buyers will never know that your item exists because they will use the eBay search engine to locate items, and a vague description in the heading is unlikely to match their search terms.

It is generally considered better to use a long heading because this makes your listing larger and more obvious in a list of search results. It also means that you can use plenty of words in the heading, thus increasing your chances of matching the search terms used by people using the eBay search engine. Obviously things should not be taken to excess, and it is not possible to have really long headings anyway, because eBay limits the number of characters that can be used.

A good way of going about things is to write down any search terms that you might use if you were looking for an item like the one you have for sale. Try to use all of them, or failing that as many as possible of them, in the heading. Make sure that any really important search criteria are included. With an ornament for example, it will probably have a maker, a name for that particular piece, and possibly some form of maker's number such as a catalogue number. Ideally these should all be included in the heading, and they should certainly be included in the main text of the listing.

If an object is in particularly fine condition it is probably best to indicate this in the heading. If it is in bad condition it is not really necessary to mention this fact in the heading, but it should obviously be made clear in the description. If it is faulty then this should definitely be indicated in the heading. As pointed out in Chapter 1, eBay now has more than just "new" and "used" options in the Condition menu when listing items, and there is one specifically for faulty items. Make sure that you use this one where appropriate, and not the "used" one.

It is acceptable to list an item as "used" when it has a minor fault that does not prevent it from being fully usable, but the flaw must be clearly detailed in the item's description. With anything like this I always highlight the section of text that describes the fault by having it in bold text, coloured red, or both. This way the buyer cannot reasonably claim that he or she did not notice a description of the fault in the listing. Do not try to scam buyers by briefly mentioning one or more faults in the middle of a deliberately overlong description! This type of thing will soon get you "into hot water" and could soon leave you with feedback that will deter many would-be bidders.

Description

Do include a proper description, and do not simply leave this blank or use something so vague that it is of no real use to potential buyers. Make sure that potential buyers know exactly what you have on offer. Where appropriate state the colour, size, or whatever. Size is especially important with items that are made in more than one size, and this does not just apply to clothes. Numerous products, including ornaments, toys, and camera bags are often produced in more than one size. With some items there is no way potential customers can know the size unless you give dimensions in the description. If you do not specify the size there is a risk that your customer will jump to conclusions. There will be trouble if your customer expects to receive a vase that is half a metre high and they receive one the size of a thimble!

Try to give a description that will give people a good idea of an item's condition. Try to be honest and give an accurate description. Do not "gloss over" or omit any mention of bad points, but it is also a mistake to list lots of tiny imperfections. This will make the item sound much worse that it is, and will deter potential bidders. A more vague description is acceptable and is all that most potential bidders require. Something along the lines of "it has some general wear, mainly on the back, in the form of a few superficial scratches" is all that is needed. Ideally the description should be backed up by some photographs of adequate quality to show the condition of the item.

Any significant damage should be mentioned, and if at all possible it should be clearly visible in one of the photographs as well. Be careful with the wording. Something can be described as "almost perfect" if it is in fantastic condition apart from a tiny scratch. It could also be described as "slightly damaged". The first description should bring in plenty of bidders whereas the second one is likely to put people off bidding at all. It is important to take this type of thing very seriously when selling relatively expensive items. The difference it could make to the maximum bid price obtained is potentially massive. You could end up wasting listing fees, or worse still, selling a few hundred pounds worth of goods at a fraction of their true value.

It is a matter of trying to emphasise the good points rather than the bad ones while not going so far as to be misleading. If an item is rare or unusual in some way, make sure that this is mentioned in the description. Mention anything that makes the item more desirable and valuable than most other objects of that type. Avoid the temptation to hype things by using words such as rare, legendary, etc., when they are actually unexceptional. On many occasions I have seen cameras described as rare, even though there were a dozen or more of them listed on eBay at the time! It is unlikely that you will fool anyone, and this type of thing immediately gives most of the potential buyers the impression that you are dishonest. If the heading or description is misleading, then you are being dishonest.

Starting price

If you opt to sell an item using a straightforward auction it is not necessary to set a price for your item. The bidders will determine the final price, although you still have to set the starting price. It is not possible to set a reserve price of less than fifty pounds, which is clearly an unrealistically high level for many of the items sold on eBay. However, it is possible to set the starting price anywhere from a few pence to many thousands of pounds, making it possible to use the starting price as a sort of pseudo reserve figure on an item.

It is only fair to point out that using a high starting price is not necessarily a good way of doing things. If you have watched auction programmes on the television you will probably be well aware that some items sell for much more than expected, while others do quite badly and in some cases do not even attract a single bid. While using a high starting price does ensure that you do not end up selling the item for next to nothing, it can also have the effect of deterring would-be bidders. Using a low starting price together with a reserve often seems to produce the same result, with many bidders being put off and not bothering to place a bid.

Using a low start

A very low starting price of 99 pence is usually the best approach with popular items that are in demand. Higher starting prices cost more, so a 99 pence start helps to minimise your listing fees. A low starting price also attracts bidders, with the bargain hunters bidding early and the serious bidders coming in towards the end. This can give an auction a sort of momentum, and a low starting price usually gives better results than a high initial price. EBay used to offer free listing days on auctions starting at 99 pence or less in an attempt to encourage people to use this way of doing things. EBay has now taken this idea a step further, and these days most auctions starting at 99 pence or less have a basic listing fee that is free. This only applies to private individuals incidentally, and not those with business accounts.

A low starting price is not always a good idea, and it can be disastrous with less popular items. You will end up selling your item for 99 pence if there are only two bidders interested in it and one of them forgets to bid! There are two ways of avoiding a disastrously low selling price, and one is to set a starting price equal to the lowest price at which you would be reasonably happy to sell the item. The other is to not use an auction format listing at all, but to use a Buy-it-Now type instead. In other words, use a listing that is effectively a straightforward second-hand advertisement where you set a selling price. Either way there is a risk that the item will not sell, but this is better than selling a rare and valuable item for a few pounds or for a matter of pence. If the pricing is fair, items that do not sell at the first attempt will often do so if they are relisted. There is normally only one listing fee to pay if a relisted item sells at the second attempt, but there are some exceptions.

There are variations on these two approaches, including one that combines the two, with a fairly high starting price being used together with a Buy-it-Now option at a slightly higher price. Do not bother trying to combine a low starting price with a high Buy-it-Now price. The Buy-it-Now option disappears when the first bid is placed, or when the reserve price is met in the case of an auction that has a reserve in place. If you use a low starting price and no reserve there will always be a joker who places an early and very low bid. This seems to be pure mischief making and is done to specifically remove the Buy-it-Now option. There is usually no intention to make a serious bid at a later time.

This is one situation where a reserve can be used to good effect, as it can protect the Buy-it-Now option from mischievous bidders. However, bear in mind that there is a 50 pound minimum for a reserve value. Also, unlike most other types of auction, there is an extra charge for using a reserve on an eBay auction, and this adds significantly to the cost of the listing. A high starting price also increases the listing fee for an item, so it makes economic sense to use one or the other rather than both.

There is an advantage in using a reserve, which is that it acts as a sort of pseudo bidder with a bid just below the reserve price. Anyone placing a bid at or above the reserve price will become the highest bidder at the reserve price. They will win the item at that price if no other bids are placed. Normally you need two obliging bidders in order to obtain a high price, but this is not the case when a reserve is used, with the reserve effectively acting as an initial high bidder.

Despite this potential advantage it is generally best to avoid using reserves, which tend to be an expensive way of putting off would-be bidders. I do not know the reason for it, but many people seem to avoid eBay auctions that have a reserve price. Possibly they feel that an item with a reserve price will have a high reserve, and that there is no point in bidding. Many items that have a reserve price do seem to have the price set unrealistically high and do not sell. Perhaps it is just that prospective buyers feel that having a reserve placed on an item removes the possibility of a bargain being obtained, and so they do not place a bid. It is worth bearing in mind that although eBay does not show the reserve price of an item, there is nothing to stop the seller from stating it in the description and (or) heading. If your reserve price is reasonable it might be worthwhile including it in the listing.

The right price

It is important to be realistic when setting a Buy-it-now or high auction starting price. If you set the price too high it is possible that you will get lucky and someone will be mug enough to buy it at that price, but it is more likely that you will end up spending a lot of money listing and relisting the item. You need to avoid making the opposite mistake where something is listed using the Buy-it-Now option, and sells within about 30 seconds because you have set the price way below the true value of the item. Anything you sell on eBay, or anywhere else, is worth what someone will pay for it, and not what you would like them to pay for it. Setting fanciful prices on things is folly, and selling things at a fraction of their true market value is plain daft.

The obvious way of finding a realistic price for an item is to search for completed listings for similar items. Using the eBay search facility, including looking for completed listings was covered in the previous chapter. Looking at completed listings to find out how much you should bid for an item and looking at completed listings to find a suitable asking price are essentially the same. Consequently, the eBay search facility will not be considered in detail here.

However, an important point to bear in mind is that you must carefully read the item descriptions. Do not settle for quickly scanning the prices in completed listings. With most items there is a huge difference in the price paid for a well worn item and one that is in mint condition. An item that it damaged, faulty, or does not include essential accessories would probably be much cheaper than one that was well worn but complete, had no major damage, and was fully working. What you are looking for is two or three items that are truly comparable to the item you are selling. These should give you a good idea of your item's real value.

Rare commodities

Valuing anything that is genuinely rare is notoriously difficult. You can search eBay for details of completed listings, but with something that is truly out of the ordinary it is likely that you will not find any listings for the same item, or even one that is very similar. There are books that try to assist with valuations for goods of various types, and there are web sites that provide price guides. You can also do a general search of the web for something that might give some useful guidance. With something rare you might not find any reliable guides to the value of your item.

No doubt we are all familiar with the television programmes where people buy things from antiques fairs or retailers and then try to sell them at auction for a profit. The often given advice is that they should buy things that are unusual. The reason for this is that with "run of the mill" items the price is well defined because goods of that type come up for sale quite frequently. The retail price tends to be higher than the auction price, so buying ordinary items from a retailer and selling at auction more or less guarantees that a loss will be made.

Accurately valuing rare and unusual items is more or less impossible as there is little or no data to act as a guide. There might be no bids for a rare item, but the price could "go through the roof" if two or more people were determined to buy it. Contestants who buy unusual items might "lose their shirts", but if they buy the goods at reasonably low prices they are in with a chance of making a good profit. When you sell something rare and unusual on eBay you are, like the contestants in the auction competitions, "in the lap of the gods". The item might flop, make a great deal of money, or anything between these two extremes.

Do not make the common mistake of assuming that something is valuable because it is rare. Prices are usually set by supply and demand, with prices rising when demand outstrips supply, and falling when supply outstrips demand. Rarity aids high prices since it means that supply will be limited, but it is still necessary to have some determined buyers in order to produce high selling prices. It does not matter how rare something is, or what merits it might have. Unless there is reasonably strong demand it will be worth little or nothing.

Probably the best approach with an unusual item is to decide what it is worth to you. Then use a reserve or starting price that ensures it will not sell for less than that price. If it does not sell, then keep it, and perhaps try to sell it at a later date. The situation is much easier if you no longer wish to keep an item, and it is genuinely of no value to you. Simply set a low starting price and accept whatever final price is achieved, be it good or bad. Binning it is probably the best course of action should no one place a bid!

Do not get conned

Although most people probably think that it is buyers on eBay that are most at risk from various scams, with the current eBay system there is very little risk for buyers of most goods provided they pay using PayPal and go through the official eBay channels. The situation is similar for sellers if payment is made via PayPal, and many sellers will now only accept payment via PayPal. If you accept some other form of payment it is important to ensure that it has fully cleared before you part with the goods. Cash on collection might seem to be safe enough, but using counterfeit money to buy second-hand goods is a common way for crooks to unload their dodgy money. It is better to insist on payment by cheque or PayPal in advance, and to only allow collection of the goods once payment has cleared.

Dubious offers

When you list something on eBay, particularly if it has a low starting price, you will almost certainly receive either offers to buy it immediately, or requests for a Buy-it-Now price. The people making these offers will sometimes come up with supposedly good reasons why they cannot wait until the end of the auction, such as they will shortly be going away on holiday. The vast majority of these messages are from people trying to buy the item at a fraction of its true value, which is why you should ignore them and let the auction run its course. Never be enticed into dealing outside eBay by one of these messages.

Make Offer button

When a Buy-it-Now listing is used on eBay there is the option of having a facility that enables people to submit an offer if they feel that the Buy-it-Now price is a little too high. This feature is only available on a Buy-it-Now listing, and not on one that is an ordinary auction listing that includes a Buy-it-now option. I have used Buy-it-Now listings with the optional Make Offer button, but I always list the item without this feature first. If the item fails to sell I either reduce the price slightly and relist it, or relist it at the same price but with the Make Offer button added.

Strangely, the item often sells at the full asking price when the Make Offer button is added. Possibly the buyers are worried that the item will be bought by someone else while their offer is being considered, so they simply dive straight in and buy it immediately. Perhaps they do not notice the Make Offer button or simply cannot be bothered using it. Anyway, it is worth using this feature when it is proving difficult to get your original asking price for an item, but it is probably best not to use it initially.

A ploy used by some professional sellers is to use a rather high asking price together with a Make Offer button. I presume that the idea is to give would-be buyers an inflated notion of an item's value in the hope that they will make an offer that is much lower than the asking price, but is still equal to or higher than its true value. In fact the idea of this method is almost certainly to entice buyers into making offers that are well above the normal market value of the item. The problem with this method is that it seems to be a slow way of selling things, and you could easily end up listing an item over and over again with no guarantee that it will eventually be sold. Apart from the wasted time and effort, the listing fees will start to add up over a period of time. Even if the item does eventually sell at a high price, the listing fees incurred could mean that the effective price obtained was actually poor to middling.

When listing an item with the Make Offer button there is the option of having bids above a certain price automatically accepted, and those below a certain price automatically declined. These are set up separately, so if preferred you can use one or the other rather than both. It is a good idea to make use of this facility since it can save time having to deal with offers that are clearly too low to be of interest, or offers that you would definitely be prepared to accept because they are quite close to the asking price. Be careful when setting it up though, as mistakes could result in items being sold well below your minimum acceptable price!

You might need to quickly reconsider the price you are asking if a few offers come in within a minute or two of your item being listed. This probably indicates that the price has been set too low, and that some experienced eBay users have immediately homed-in on your listing. They are trying to see if they can obtain the item at an even lower price via the offer system. If their offers are not accepted it is quite likely that one of them will use the Buy-it-Now button and buy the item at the full price. Rather than accepting one of the offers you should wait to see if the item sells at the full price. If, on reflection, you consider that the offer price has been set too low, you probably have a matter of minutes or even seconds in which to amend the listing and set a better asking price!

Piece by piece

When selling a group of objects it is generally better if they are sold individually rather than being sold together as an outfit or a collection. Selling a group of things is clearly much less work than selling them individually, but the extra work involved when selling them separately is likely to be well rewarded. The problem with selling a group of items is that there will be a limited number of people who require every object in the group.

Many of your potential buyers will already have certain things in the group, and will have little or no use for these items that duplicate what they already have. Other potential buyers, although very interested in one or two of the items, will simply have no interest at all in the others. This results in a significant number of potential buyers not bidding at all, or placing low bids because they are basing their bid price only on the items that interest them, and not on the full set of items.

Many dealers make a living from eBay by buying sets of items at relatively low prices, and then selling them individually at much higher prices. They are in effect making a living from the laziness or ineptitude of other sellers on eBay. It is up to you to decide whether it is worth putting in the extra effort to sell items individually, or to save time and effort by selling them together, and probably make a dealer very happy as well. I suppose that with cheap items the amount of extra money gained from selling them individually might not be very great. Also, selling items separately usually results in slightly higher fees being paid to eBay. Any extra money obtained might not be sufficient to justify the extra work involved. A great deal of extra time might be involved if the items have to be posted to the buyers, which is quite likely to be the case. With relatively expensive things it is usually well worthwhile selling the items separately, and the extra time involved is almost certain to be well rewarded.

It is probably best not to take individual selling to extremes. With something like a camera outfit it usually better to sell the camera and other major items such as lenses and flashguns separately. Selling small accessories separately is less worthwhile, since it involves a lot of extra time but is likely to bring in very little extra money. In fact it can be difficult to sell inexpensive accessories at all. I suppose that there is little incentive for buyers to seek second-hand bargains when they can buy the items new at quite low prices. Most buyers probably just buy them new and never even consider looking for good second-hand equivalents.

It is probably best to include small accessories with the major item they are used with. This helps to make the major items more attractive to potential buyers, and might help to produce a better final selling price. It pays to "do your homework" on the prices of the major items in case some of them turn out to be worth much less than you originally estimated. Again taking a photographic example, many electronic flashguns that were quite expensive a few years ago now have very little value because they are not compatible with the latest cameras. It might be better to include a flashgun of this type with the camera body instead of trying to sell it separately.

Current value

This would definitely be worth considering if the camera was one that, like the flashgun, had fallen in value and was worth relatively little. Unfortunately, many technology products soon become superseded and their second-hand prices then tumble. The value of others can fluctuate due to changes in fashion. Do not make the mistake of valuing items on the basis of the sum you paid for them, particularly if you bought them several years ago. It is the market value of the item when you place your listing with eBay that counts, and not the price paid years earlier.

There may be other factors to take into account. In general, with collectable and antique items, the prices paid at some form of retail outlet are higher than the prices reached at auction. In fact a fair percentage of the items on offer in the retail outlets are bought at auction. It is for this reason that most of the contestants tend to do rather badly in the television programs where they try to make a profit by buying from retailers and selling at auction. They are "swimming against the tide", and using a method of buying and selling that on average is more or less guaranteed to produce losses. Most of the goods sold by private buyers on eBay have probably been bought from a retail outlet of some sort, and are likely to sell for significantly less than the prices paid by the sellers. Of course, there will usually be a substantial loss when selling practically any goods that were bought new, even if they are still almost new.

Trying to sell items at the price you would like to receive instead of the current going rate is a common mistake. You cannot force a high price onto an item. It will sell for the price that potential buyers are prepared to pay, and not what you feel the item is worth. Trying to sell goods at grossly inflated prices will usually result in no sale being obtained, and the eBay listing fees mounting up. It is probably best to keep an item if its current market price is well below its value to you.

Breaking up

While selling major items separately will usually get you the best total price, selling a major item and its relatively minor accessories separately is probably not a good idea. A digital camera for example, usually comes complete with various accessories when bought new. These include such things as a rechargeable battery, battery charger, a software disc, and possibly other items such as a case. These could be sold separately, but it would require more time and effort, and would probably produce a lower total price than selling the items as a single lot.

The problem with selling the accessories separately is that it can severely reduce the price obtained for the main item, and could make it difficult to sell at all. An item without its accessories will be popular with buyers who have a non-working example and with those who have lost the main item or had it stolen. They will still have the accessories and would probably be willing to buy a "bare" replacement unit. However, they will be looking to buy at a significant discount, as they would otherwise be better off buying a complete outfit and having a spare set of accessories.

People wishing to buy a complete outfit are unlikely to be interested in the main item without its essential bits and pieces. They will not be interested in buying the main unit and then having to go in search of the accessories needed to make it work. At least, they might be prepared to do this, but only if the main unit is at a knock-down price that will make it worth their while doing so. There is no point in selling the items separately if the main unit has to be sold off cheaply.

Boxing clever

Although to some extent it depends on the type of item concerned, most items sell more easily and at higher prices if they are complete with the original box, and where appropriate, any internal packaging as well. I suppose that with a nearly new item it is nice for buyers to have the item much as it was when originally purchased, complete with the box. The inclusion of the box, provided it is in good condition, will also help to give the impression that the item is in new condition. Accordingly, in general they will bid a little higher.

It is actually with older items, and especially many types of collectable goods, that the inclusion of the box will give the greatest increase in price. Collectable toys are perhaps the best example of this phenomenon, but it probably applies to any collectable goods that were originally supplied in a box. Things like original instruction manuals and sales receipts might also help to bolster the price. Anyway, if you still have the box for an item you are selling, it should be included in the auction, even if it means delving around in the loft to find it. Remember to mention the box in the item description, and to feature it in the photograph that shows everything included in the sale. Particularly with collectable items, it is worth mentioning the box in the listings heading.

Searching

Whether you are buying or selling, the importance of the eBay search facility is something that should not be underestimated. When buying items on eBay you need a means of quickly finding suitable candidates amongst the millions of items listed on the eBay sites. It is also advisable to look at completed auctions for items of the type that you are interested in buying. This will provide a good guide to the type of price you will have to pay for each one. A rethink will be necessary if you are prepared to pay up to about ten pounds for an item and the lowest price for one in the recent past is about five times that figure! Either your maximum bid price has to be adjusted upwards by a substantial amount, or you will probably have to give up on the idea altogether.

The search facility is equally useful when selling goods on eBay. It is a good idea to look through the listings for items that are similar to the ones you intend to auction. Copying other peoples' listings is not allowed under eBay rules, but you might find some useful information about the items you are selling. Using this information to help sell your own items is perfectly legitimate, but do your homework on the Internet to make sure that the information is correct. Also ensure that information is relevant to the item you are selling. There are numerous instances of two virtually identical items where one sells for several times the price of the other. When selling something as a rare and unusual item you must ensure that it really is the rare, unusual, and more pricy version.

Current listings for an item you intend to auction are not usually a very good guide to its value. The fact that there are Buy-it-Now listings where the buyers are asking about one hundred pounds does not necessarily mean that it is genuinely worth something of that order. It could simply be that there are some sellers asking inflated prices in the hope of finding a mug! This is not exactly a rare phenomenon on eBay and other online auction sites.

The fact that there are active auctions where the bid price is a matter of pence or a few pounds does not necessarily mean that your item is practically worthless. As explained in some detail in Chapter 1, most of the bidding tends to take place in the few minutes or seconds of an auction, so it is not really a great surprise if most of the active auctions have quite low current bid prices, or no bids at all. Completed auctions are a much better guide to the value of items. However, looking at the current listings will at least give some idea of the quality and quantity of the competition you face.

Completed listings

When looking at completed listings to gauge the value of an item you intend to sell, or as a guide to the price you should bid as a buyer, do not be surprised if the final selling prices vary widely. With auctions there will always be some variation in the price obtained for an item of a particular type. There will even be significant variations with goods that are identical. In theory they are the same and should have the same value. However, in the real world there could be two determined bidders at one auction who inflate the price in their eagerness to buy the item. At the next auction some of the high bidders might forget to bid or be unavoidably detained so that they are unable to bid. The item would then sell at a bargain price to one of the bidders who did actually get around to placing a bid.

Larger variations in price could be due to someone making a mistake and selling the item on a Buy-it-Now basis at well below its true value. A high price could be due to the opposite of this, with someone trying to sell an item at a high price on a Buy-it-Now basis in the hope of finding a mug, and succeeding. High prices can also be produced by two bidders getting carried away and bidding an item up to a daft price, or by shill bidding. Having bid an item up to an excessive price it is quite common for the winning bidder to welsh on the deal. Shill bidding often results in the seller buying their own item! Where an auctioned item has sold for a completely "over the top" price, do not be surprised if it is relisted soon

2 Selling on eBay

Fig.2.2 It is possible to search within a main category

afterwards. Do not be misled by high prices that for one reason or another are decidedly dodgy.

Large variations in the price for similar items are most likely to be due to differences in condition, or perhaps due to something important being missing from items that have sold cheaply. The feedback rating of the seller can adversely affect the selling price, as can a listing that looks a bit dodgy in some respect. The final prices obtained for goods can therefore be a bit misleading unless you read the item description to see if there are any factors responsible for an abnormally high or low price. The completed listings that are most useful are the ones that are placed by reliable buyers, and that are for an item that is in every respect very much like the one you have for sale.

Search types

There are two basic search methods when using eBay, and one of these is much like using an ordinary search engine such as Google. One or more search terms are typed into the Search textbox which is situated

Selling on Ebay 2

Fig.2.3 A main category can be selected from this menu

near the top of most eBay pages, and the Search button is operated. The default is for the entire site to be searched, but it is possible to restrict the search to one of the main eBay categories using the drop-down menu (Figure 2.2).

The alternative approach is to browse an entire category, or a sub-category. There is a menu on the eBay homepage (Figure 2.3) that enables a full menu of main categories to be obtained (Figure 2.4). Selecting one of these provides a list of the items in that sub-category (Figure 2.5). The normal search facility is available via the textbox, etc., near the top of the page, so it is possible to search within a sub-category.

A whole range of filters becomes available once a list of items is displayed. Most of the filters in the left-hand column are based on information provided by the sellers when filling out the listing forms, but the one from completed listings will also be found here. Some of these filters can be helpful at removing items that are of no interest and concentrating on those that are, but the system is not foolproof. Some sellers do not bother to tick the checkboxes when listing their items, which can result in them being missed from some filtered searches. Other sellers are

2 Selling on eBay

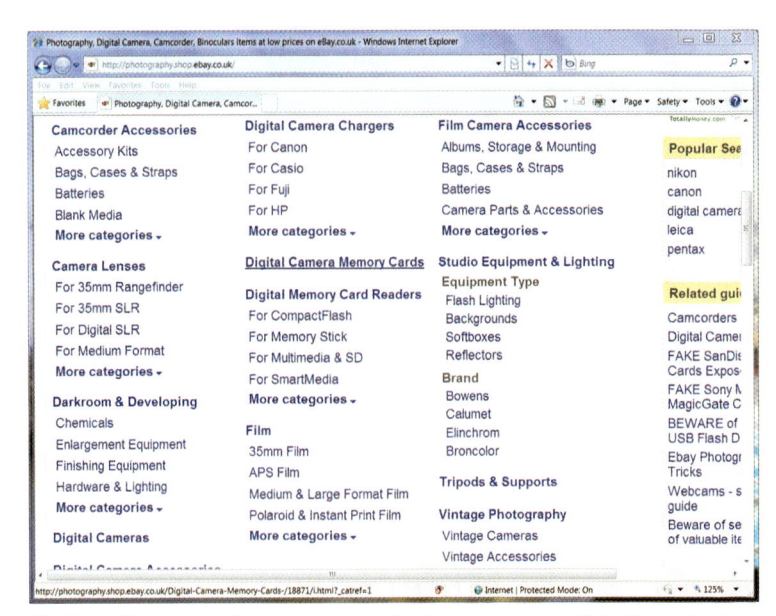

Fig.2.4 This page shows a menu of sub-categories within the selected main category

either a bit careless or do not understand the terminology when completing this section of the listing form.

This can result in their items sometimes being omitted from matching types of filtered search, and appearing in searches where they are inappropriate. The lesson for sellers here is that the relevant parts of the listing form should always be filled in completely and as accurately as possible. There is otherwise a strong likelihood that some potential bidders will miss your listings, which could have an adverse effect on the selling prices.

The lesson for buyers is that you cannot totally rely on these filters, and that manually going through a subsection, although laborious, is more reliable. It pays to bear in mind that any search is reliant on the seller getting it right, with items being listed in an appropriate subsection, suitable words being used in the item headings, everything in the heading being spelled correctly and so on. Carelessness when listing items can make it difficult for potential buyers to find them, and could cost you a lot of money.

Selling on Ebay 2

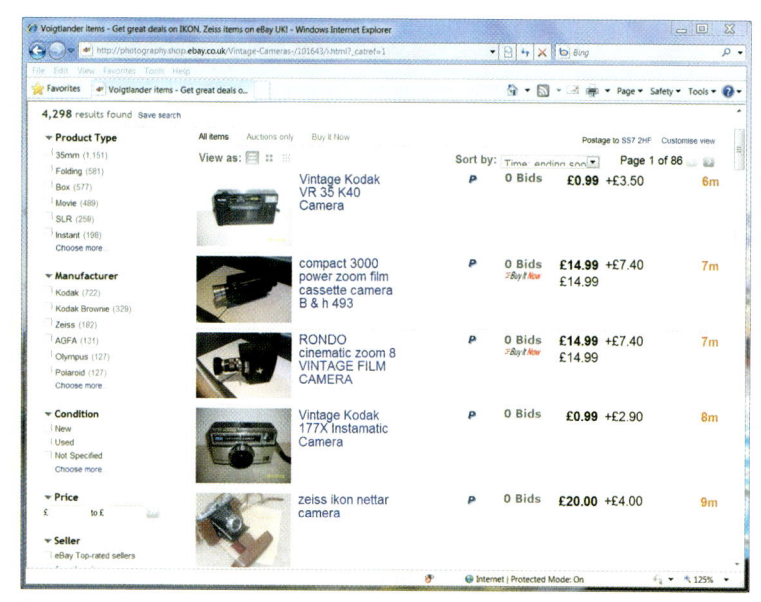

Fig.2.5 A list of items within one of the sub-categories

Sort by

When a list of items is displayed there will be a Sort by menu somewhere near the top right-hand corner of the page (Figure 2.6). This enables further filtering to be added, or changes the way results are displayed. The top two options in the menu are the most popular, and they simply control the

Fig.2.6 Results can be listed in various ways

order in which results are displayed. One of these options is "Time: newly listed". Having newly listed items displayed first is useful when

71

2   Selling on eBay

Fig.2.7 You can view all listings, auctions, or Buy-it-Now listings

regularly checking to see if there are any new items of interest. The "Time: ending soonest" option is useful when you need to know if there are any items of interest that are ending soon, and might be worth bidding on.

Most of the other options relate to price, postage rates and whether items are new or second-hand. To some extent these duplicate the facilities available in the left-hand column of the page. The "Best Match" option is a relatively new one, and it is the option used by default. It seems to be primarily intended for use with Buy-it-Now listings rather than auctions. You can opt to see all listings, only Buy-it-Now listings, or only auction listings using the three tabs near the top of each search page (Figure 2.7). Normal auctions with a Buy-it-Now button will appear whichever of the tabs is selected.

The "Best Match" name is perhaps a bit misleading, since it does not seem to have anything to do with how well your search terms match the titles of listings. The normal search criteria seem to apply, but listings from sellers with good ratings appear near the top of the search list, while those with poor ratings are placed near the bottom. Presumably it is the "Best Match" in the sense that the first results you see are from the best sellers that match your search terms. When applied to auction listing the order of the search results seems to be based on a combination of seller ratings and the time left until the end of the auction. The "Best Match" option is very laudable in theory, but I cannot say that I have ever found it to be of any great value in practice. The two time based search orders seem to be far more useful.

Matching mistakes

Sometimes when you search for something on eBay you find that there are no matching results. This could simply be because there are

Selling on Ebay 2

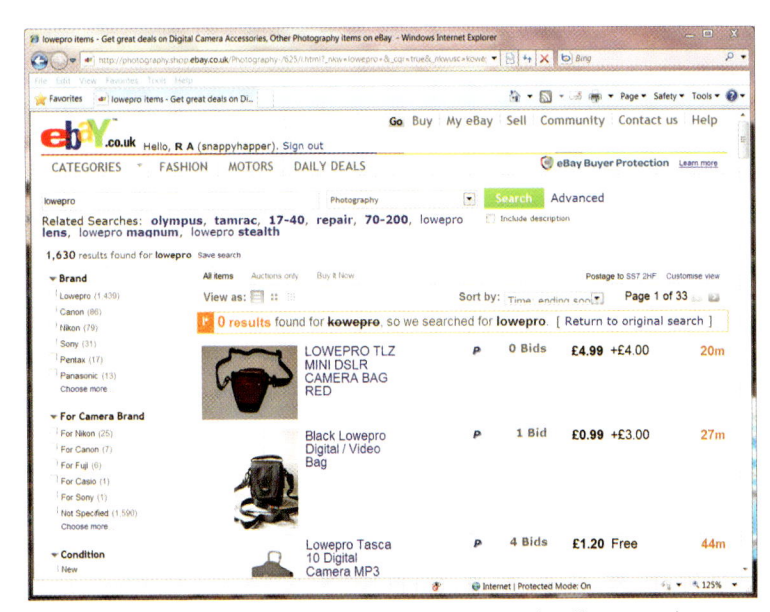

Fig.2.8 The search engine might make a suggestion if no matches are found

genuinely no goods of the type you require currently listed, or it could be due to you making an error in one of the search terms. If you check the search terms and everything seems to be correct, it is possible that you think that you know how to spell something correctly, but you are actually making a mistake. The eBay search facility, in common with most modern search engines, will sometimes make a suggestion if it thinks you might have made a mistake. In the example of Figure 2.8 the search engine has gone a stage further. I used "kowepro" instead of "lowepro" as the sole search term when searching for a camera bag in the Lowepro range. The search engine could not find a match for my search term, but it found plenty for "lowepro" and has listed those instead.

There are programs and web sites that are specifically designed to find matches even when either you have made a mistake, or there are errors in the headings of listings. The Goofbay site featured in Chapter 1 has a facility of this type that can be accessed via the Misspelled Search link on the homepage (refer back to Figure 1.29 in Chapter 1). Operating this link produces the page of Figure 2.9, where there are numerous search criteria that can be used. However, the textbox for the search terms (Keywords) is the only one that it is essential to use.

2 Selling on eBay

Fig.2.9 Various search criteria are available, but most are optional

For this example I used the correct name of "lowepro" and accepted the default settings. By default the search engine ignores exact matches, and instead looks for words that are almost right but not quite. An impressive 48 "near misses" were found (Figure 2.10), although only about one third of these were listings for Lowepro camera bags. These were mostly where the name had been misspelled as "Lowpro". This type of search engine can be used for various reasons, but its main purpose is to find ineptly listed items that most buyers will miss, and that are likely to sell at a low price as a result of this.

Erase personal data

In recent years there have been numerous news stories about personal data and even secret government information found on the hard disc drives of second-hand computers. These demonstrate the importance of ensuring that all your data is erased before parting with any mass storage device you are selling, or any gadget that contains a mass storage device of some kind. Bear in mind that erasing data does not usually

Selling on Ebay 2

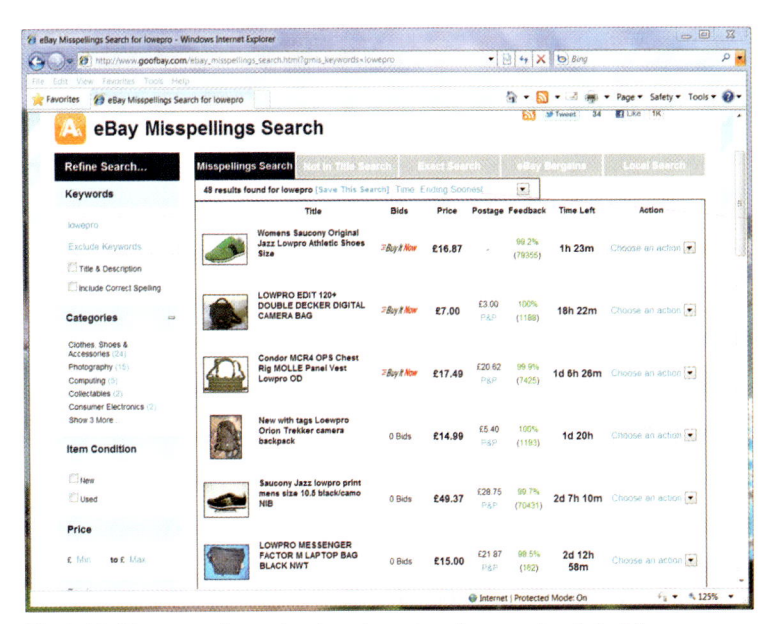

Fig.2.10 The search engine has found an impressive list of items

result in it being totally wiped from the hard disc drive. In fact it does not usually result in any of the data being erased at all. What usually happens is that the entries for files are removed from the file allocation table, which is a type of database that the computer uses to find files on the disc. With a file's entry removed from the database, as far as the computer is concerned the file no longer exists.

However, there are utility programs that can be used to recover erased files provided they have not been overwritten by new files. This is great if you accidentally erase some files and need to recover them, but it also has a downside. It means that erasing files before you sell a storage device does not guarantee that the buyer of the equipment will not be able to examine them. Just the opposite in fact, and should the buyer of the equipment wish to do so, they will be able to recover and examine all the files.

In order to render the files unrecoverable it is necessary to first delete them and then copy unimportant files to the hard disc drive until the drive is full. Then delete these files. Anyone using software to recover the deleted files on the disc will then recover the unimportant files used to fill the disc, and not your data files. There are file shredding and disc cleaning utility programs available that will do the job for you, and most of these will overwrite existing files several times so that even the most sophisticated of file recovery techniques will be unable to resurrect your personal data files.

Keep in mind that any form of storage device has the potential to give others your personal data, and it is not only hard disc drives that need to be properly "wiped" before they are sold. Some of the stories about lost data that have hit the headlines in recent years have been revolved around memory cards rather than hard disc drives. The capacities of modern memory cards are measured in gigabytes rather than megabytes, and they have the potential to give away vast amounts of your personal data.

These devices are formatted and used by computers as pseudo disc drives. As with conventional disc drives, when data is deleted from a memory card the process used does not normally involve any of the data actually being erased from the card's memory. This again makes it possible to recover deleted files that have not been overwritten by other files. Many sellers simply opt not to include memory cards with computers, cameras, etc., when selling them. If you do include a used memory card when selling an item, erase all the data it contains, fill the card with unimportant files that contain no personal data, and then delete these from the card. As with a hard disc drive, this procedure ensures that only the unimportant files can be recovered, and not your data files, which will have been overwritten.

Do not overlook any Flash memory that is built into a gadget that you are selling. I recently bought a second-hand digital camera on eBay that was not supplied with a memory card. I therefore fitted it with a brand-new card and took some test shots. When examining the test photographs I was surprised to see that the first ones displayed on the camera's display were of a car, a house, a dog, and a naked lady on a bed, none of which were taken by me! A little investigation revealed that the mystery photographs were not actually stored on the memory card, but were instead stored on the camera's internal memory and had presumably be taken by the camera's previous owner. Make sure that any memory of this type is properly "cleaned" before the gadget is sold. When selling a computer make sure that there are no discs left in CDROM or DVD drives.

Personal collection only

It is reasonable to insist that items are collected in person and to offer no delivery option with something that is very large and (or) heavy, but where it is reasonably possible to offer a delivery option you should certainly do so. eBay enables users to sell items to any part of the UK, or even on a worldwide basis. With a huge number of potential buyers, and within reason, it should be possible to obtain a good price for any item using eBay. However, if you cannot be bothered packing goods and taking them to the Post Office, and will only sell to buyers who will come and collect the goods, you will not be making the best use of eBay. Your potential pool of buyers would be about the same as when placing a small advertisement in a local newspaper.

In some cases you might actually sell the item at a reasonable price, but being realistic about matters, the selling price will nearly always be significantly higher if a delivery option is provided. With many items it is likely that the selling price will be very low or that there will be no bidders at all unless a delivery option is offered. If you are not prepared to carefully pack items and take them to the Post Office or use some other delivery company, then selling on eBay is probably not for you.

Secure packing

Inadequately packing items is a strong candidate for the most common error made by newcomers to selling items on eBay. I have received photographic equipment, including cameras and lenses, packed in large mailing bags. These bags have padding, but even on the most generous of them it is very thin and is not designed to protect delicate items that are bulky and (or) heavy. Sending something like a camera, lens, glass or porcelain ornament, or clock in nothing more than a padded mailing bag more or less guarantees that the item will arrive in a damaged state. The Post Office and other delivery companies will not reimburse you if an item is damaged in transit due to inadequate packaging.

I generally work on the assumption that during its way to the buyer an item will be dropped onto a hard floor from a height of two or three metres, and that it needs to be packed accordingly. I am probably being unduly pessimistic, but I have not yet had a problem with anything getting damaged in transit, and with this type of thing it is better to err on the side of caution. When sending expensive items it is definitely better to opt for a degree of overkill to make quite sure that the item arrives intact.

Anything delicate should be sent in a reasonably tough box that is at least 60 millimetres larger on each dimension than the item being sent. This enables at least 30 millimetres of packing material to be used around the object. With large and (or) heavy items there needs to be room for a much greater thickness of packaging. Apart from keeping the item itself much safer, plenty of extra packing reduces the risk of the item breaking through the box, and possibly getting lost in the post as a result.

While packing material can be improvised using shredded paper, screwed up newspaper, and the like, it is much better to use proper packing materials such as bubble-wrap or pieces of expanded polystyrene. With larger items the cost of proper packing could be excessive, and a mixture of the genuine article and improvised packing then offers a good compromise. It makes sense to recycle packing materials as far as possible, so it is a good idea to retain any useful packing that is used with the items you buy on eBay or when using some other form of distance selling. There are a number of eBay sellers that specialise in packing materials, and these mostly offer better deals than can be obtained locally, especially if you plan ahead and buy fairly large quantities.

Phone home

Some eBay listings have little or no item description, but instead have a request to telephone the supplied number for more details. The supplied number is usually a mobile type that could be expensive for callers. This type of thing is not popular with potential buyers, who do not really want to spend time and money calling about an item that may well be of no interest to them. It is likely that most of them will not pursue the matter further and will simply move on to the next listing. Even if the listing does provoke a large number of responses, as a seller, do you really want to spend large amounts of time answering numerous telephone calls?

The item description should always be included, and it should include a reasonable amount of information about the item for sale. There should be sufficient information for potential bidders to at least decide whether it is worth pursuing the matter further. With a complex and expensive item it might be worthwhile including a telephone number so that potential bidders can quickly clarify a number of points. Ideally, the item description should always be full and detailed. Do not bother including a telephone number with low-cost items where the cost of the call could easily be greater than the value of the goods on offer. Even where a telephone number is included in the listing, you must still be prepared to answer questions via the eBay messaging system in the usual way.

Stick by the rules

Many eBay sellers devote more space to various terms and conditions than they do to the item being sold. In fact I have seen plenty of examples where there is a vast amount of space devoted to this type of thing, with the item for sale barely being mentioned at all! Too much "red tape" will tend to put off would-be bidders, and you have to bear in mind that you are bound by the laws of the land, and also by the eBay trading rules. You cannot make up your own terms and conditions in an attempt to override either of these.

Selling abroad

In general, you can expect to receive higher prices if you are prepared to sell items outside your own country, because the pool of potential bidders is increased. However, there are a few points that need to be borne in mind if you start exporting. It is not possible to send items weighing more than 2 kilograms by Airmail. There are alternatives that can be used for heavier items, but these tend to involve more hassle and can be very expensive. Consequently, many eBay sellers will not send anything abroad if it has a packed weight of more than 2 kilograms. Having sent a couple of heavy items to Japan on a couple of occasions, I would not be willing to do anything similar again.

In most respects, selling within the European Union is not really much different to selling within one of the member countries. There are no customs forms to contend with, and for trading purposes the European Union is effectively one country. There could be a language problem, although trading on eBay does not necessarily require any communication between the buyer and the seller. It is when things go wrong that problems are more likely to arise, and sorting out problems with someone who does not understand your language could be difficult.

Remember that the cost of postage is likely to be higher when sending items to another country, especially for an expensive item that requires a signed-for service and (or) extra insurance cover. Find the approximate cost of postage for other countries before listing an item, so that you can charge a sensible amount for delivery. In fact you should do this for postage within your own country. Do not make the classic mistake of

2   Selling on eBay

underestimating the postage charge and effectively giving the item to your customer for the price of posting it to them.

When selling outside your own trading zone it is necessary to complete a customs form, and eBay has facilities for printing these. It is the responsibility of the buyer to pay any import duties on the item, and it is a good idea to include a notice to this effect on your listings. It is probably best to insist on payment using PayPal, even if you do not normally do so for sales within your own country. Other methods tend to be expensive or are simply not applicable when receiving money from abroad. In most cases the buyer and seller will both receive the protection normally provided by using PayPal for an eBay transaction.

You should be able to find a postage calculator (price finder) at www.royalmail.com

3

Photographs for eBay

Good photographs

According to the old saying "a picture is worth a thousand words", but I think it would probably be more accurate to say that "a good picture is worth a thousand words". A bad picture is probably not worth anything, and a mediocre one is perhaps worth a few hundred words. In an eBay context, a bad picture will leave potential buyers none the wiser, and a mediocre one will not be of great help. In both cases there is a risk that potential buyers will think that you are trying to hide something. This can result in them bidding less than they would otherwise be prepared to pay, or simply not bothering to bid at all.

There are two stages in getting really good photographs for your listing, which are to first take at least a reasonably competent photograph, and then to process it to optimise results. Taking bad photographs and then trying to make them good using a photo editing program is not a good approach, and is likely to produce poor to middling results. Try to take photographs that are really good to start with, and then use photo editing software to do some "fine tuning".

It is not necessary to spend large amounts of money on a photo editing program. Digital cameras are often supplied complete with basic but reasonably capable editing software, and in some cases the bundled software is actually quite sophisticated. If there is no bundled software that is up to the task it is just a matter of using a free photo editing program such as Google's Picasa or GIMP.

Taking photographs

To some extent the basic technique for photographing eBay items has to be varied to suit the item concerned. The approach for photographing something sizeable such as a car will inevitably be different to that used

3 Photographs for eBay

Fig.3.1 Backlighting tends to give a silhouette effect

when taking the picture of something small such as a gold ring. With a car you can at least wait for a nice day and park it somewhere picturesque so that it is in pleasant looking surroundings. With something like a large electrical appliance or piece of furniture you will probably have to photograph it in situ. You can still tidy up and make the surroundings look as good as possible. Most digital cameras have a zoom lens that covers from a slightly wide angle of view to a moderately telephoto type.

In general, things look better when photographed well back using a telephoto setting rather than at close quarters using a wide angle of view. The problem with the wide-angle approach is that it often results in exaggerated perspective and possibly some odd looking distortions as well. Things tend to look as though they are suffering from "middle-age spread"! Obviously there will not always be sufficient space available to use the longest focal lengths, and it is then a matter of getting as far

Photographs for eBay   **3**

Fig.3.2 Exposure compensation improves matters, but not a lot

back as possible and using the longest focal length that enables the complete object to be fitted into the picture.

Avoid backlighting

A common error is to place the subject of the picture on a table directly in front of a window where it will receive plenty of daylight. Getting plenty of light on the subject is definitely a good idea, but with the table directly in front of the window you are inevitably on the opposite side of the table to the light source. In photographic jargon the subject is "backlit", and you are "shooting into the light". Backlighting can be used to good effect in creative ways, but in the current context it is more likely to give a glaring background and a subject that is little more than a silhouette (Figure 3.1).

Fig.3.3 Some image processing produces a further improvement

Using exposure compensation to lighten the subject gives slightly better results (Figure 3.2), but tends to give a washed-out look with excessive areas of bleached highlights. With some processing of the backlit image it is possible to improve it (Figure 3.3), but it is still not very good. Results are likely to be better with the subject and the camera the other way around. In other words, you should be close to the window with the light coming from behind you, with the subject on the table which should be placed well into the room. In Figure 3.4 I have used this method together with a simple cloth background, and results are much improved. The photograph of Figure 3.3 is perhaps more dramatic, but the one of Figure 3.4 gives a better idea of what the camera actually looks like, and its condition.

Avoid camera shake

Another advantage of placing the subject well into the room is that it avoids having it in direct sunlight. While direct sunlight will give a good

Photographs for eBay 3

Fig.3.4 In general, front lighting the subject gives the best result

exposure, it also tends to give harsh shadows and high contrast. The same is true when the light source is a single flashgun. Few things look good with this type of lighting. A more diffuse light source normally gives better results. The main drawback of placing the subject well into the room is that the light level tends to be relatively low. In order to get a proper exposure the shutter speed has to be relatively long, and "camera shake" can then be a problem. In other words, slight movement of the camera during the exposure tends to blur the image, often giving an unpleasant double-image effect.

The best way of avoiding camera shake is to mount the camera on a tripod. Failing that, some cameras have some form of anti-blur facility such as an optical image stabiliser, and using a facility of this type will

3 Photographs for eBay

Fig.3.5 Although the image is not "pin" sharp, the image stabiliser has worked well

often provide good results in situations where problems with camera-shake would otherwise occur. The photographs of Figure 3.5 and 3.6 show the improvement that some form of image stabiliser can make when the circumstances are right. Bear in mind the limitations of these systems though. The photographs will be very blurred if a really long shutter time has to be used, with or without the use of an image stabiliser.

With modern cameras it is usually possible to set the sensitivity (ISO) setting quite high, and this gives good shutter speeds even with quite dim lighting. Using a high ISO setting tends to give "noisy" pictures where plain areas of the image have a grainy look. However, in the current context this will probably not be a problem. The grainy look tends to largely disappear when the high definition photographs are reduced to the much lower definition pictures used in the eBay listing.

Using flash

Fig.3.6 The image is totally blurred if it is taken without the aid of the stabiliser

Using the camera's built-in flashgun will normally avoid camera-shake, because the pulse of light from the gun is very brief and it effectively gives a very short shutter time. It is typically equivalent to a shutter speed of one thousandth of a second or less. The very blurred photograph of Figure 3.7 was taken using the available light and a long shutter time, while the one of Figure

Photographs for eBay   **3**

Fig.3.7 Long shutter times produce very blurred results

3.8 was taken with the aid of the camera's built-in flashgun. The difference between the two is very apparent.

However, as explained previously, flash lighting tends to be quite harsh and it does not always give particularly good results. Using a flashgun

Fig.3.8 Using flash lighting has produced a sharp image

87

3 Photographs for eBay

Fig.3.9 Shiny surfaces and flash lighting can produce some very harsh looking results

built into the camera often gives problems with the light from the flashgun being reflected back to the camera from shiny surfaces, giving very bright areas and problems with glare and excessive contrast (Figure 3.9). With flat surfaces that are highly reflective it is usually better if none of these surfaces are perpendicular to the camera. This avoids having much of the light reflected straight back at the camera, and instead results in it being reflected to one side of the camera.

Problems with glare can be greatly reduced even with the camera moved only slightly away from the perpendicular. This is demonstrated by Figure 3.10, where the angle of the taking camera to the one being photographed is not much different to that used in Figure 3.9, but the amount of glare has been significantly reduced. The texture surface on the subject matter is much more apparent in Figure 3.10. Using a greater angle when photographing a shiny object using flash can result in it appearing very dark, although some processing using an image editor will usually improve matters.

The flash photograph of Figure 3.11 required some processing, but in the processed image the front of the camera looks quite reasonable. However, the highly polished silver top plate looks black! In fact it appears to be black in all the flash photographs of this camera. The darkening

Photographs for eBay 3

Fig.3.10 A slight change of shooting angle can give an improvement

Fig.3.11 With too great an angle things can look a little dark

3   Photographs for eBay

Fig.3.12 Using available light and no flash usually gives the best results with highly reflective objects

effect is presumably caused by most of the light from the flashgun being reflected away from the taking camera. One way around this is to have someone hold something like a large sheet of white paper so that as "seen" by the taking camera, it is reflected in the subject matter. The reflection of something light in colour is usually sufficient to brighten the subject without introducing problematic amounts of glare.

In general though, shiny objects tend to look best when taken using well diffused available light, and it is probably worth waiting for a bright day before photographing awkward subjects such as this. The photograph of Figure 3.12 was taken using the available light method, but despite my best efforts the top of the camera still looks a little dull. It at least looks more silver than black! Of the four photographs of this camera, it is this one that probably gives the best impression of what the subject actually looks like.

Fill-in flash

Results with flash are generally better if you can get a reasonable amount of light onto the subject and then use the flashgun as well. A mixture of flash and available light, with the flashgun acting as the main light source, usually gives much better results than using the flashgun as the sole

Photographs for eBay 3

Fig.3.13 Using fill-in flash can give almost shadow-free images

light source. The natural light softens the shadows and gives a more pleasing result. Similarly, the light from the flashgun softens the shadows produced by the natural light. The exact effect obtained depends on the relative strengths of the two light sources.

Flash lighting can also be useful if you cannot avoid having a backlit subject. The light from the flashgun gives a better balance between the subject and the bright background, and should avoid the silhouette problem described previously. This technique is known as "fill-in" flash.

The photograph of Figure 3.13 was taken using a combination of natural light and light from a flashgun. Figure 3.14 shows the same shot taken purely with the available light, and while it is not too bad, there are some fairly strong shadows, particularly in places down the left edge of the image. At the other extreme, the picture is overexposed and "bleached out" in the top right-hand corner. The light from the flashgun has reduced these problems, but it has not been made so strong that it starts to introduce strong shadows of its own.

Fig.3.14 The available light version of Fig.3.13. This version has more obvious shadows and is excessively bright in the top right-hand corner

Most modern digital cameras have the ability to use fill-in flash, but with the more basic models the user generally has only limited or no control over the effect obtained. It will often be necessary to use the forced flash mode, which is the one where the flashgun is always fired, even if the camera's exposure system considers that there is sufficient natural light and that the flashgun is not needed. The manual for your camera should have a section dealing with fill-in flash and the use of balanced flash/ daylight techniques.

Note that a combination of natural and flash light is only likely to work well if the natural light is reasonably strong. Otherwise the shutter speed tends to be quite long in order to obtain an adequate amount of exposure from the available light. This can result in a sharp image from the flash light combined with a blurred image from the available light, and a very odd looking soft-focus effect.

Fig.3.15 This image was taken using a flashgun fitted with a diffuser

Diffuser

Images can also look slightly odd when taking photographs using flash as the sole light source. The flashgun is usually just above the camera's lens, and it is often slightly offset to one side. The shadows produced by this arrangement are usually in the form of thin dark lines that appear mainly underneath objects and to one side. Shooting small objects at short distance tends to broaden the shadows slightly, but the photographs still tend to have a harsh and unnatural look.

It is usually possible to remove the shadows using a photo editing program, but this can be a time consuming process and it is not always a practical proposition. The balanced approach to flash and natural light described previously is a better solution, but again, it is not always a practical proposition. Another approach is to use a flashgun fitted with a large diffuser, or a "light modifier" as these devices are sometimes called. The photographs of Figures 3.13 and 3.14 show a flashgun fitted with one of these devices.

The idea is simply to increase the size of the light source, which makes shadows larger but less dark. In this way the black lining effect is avoided, and photographs generally look much better with this type of light source instead of the "raw" light from the flashgun. The photograph of Figure 3.15 was taken using a diffuser on the flashgun, and it certainly has a more natural look than most close-up flash shots. Adding one of these devices reduces the intensity of the light, but a reduction in the maximum flash intensity is unlikely to be a problem when photographing relatively small items at short distances.

Unfortunately, a large diffuser is impractical with a built-in flashgun, which is probably the type that most people use when taking photographs for use in eBay listings. These days only the more upmarket cameras can take an external flashgun, and the flashguns themselves are quite expensive. Even where the use of an external flashgun is possible, most users settle for the cheaper option of using the built-in flashgun. It took nearly two thousand pounds worth of equipment to take the photograph of Figure 3.15!

However, it is possible to obtain a similar effect with a little improvisation. Getting a helper to hold a large piece of white paper above the subject can be quite effective. The paper reflects the light from the flashgun down onto the subject, which can give a good fill-in lighting effect. It will probably require a bit of experimentation in order to obtain optimum results, but there is the potential for results to be even better than those produced using a separate flashgun and a diffuser.

Close-ups (macro)

Items for sale on eBay are often quite small, and while small might be beautiful, for the photographer small is difficult. Most digital cameras have a so-called "macro" mode that enables the camera to focus accurately at much smaller distances than can normally be accommodated. Unfortunately, the macro facility usually operates in a rather unhelpful way, with the greatest macro magnification being possible at the wide-angle end of the lens's zoom range. As explained previously, there can be problems with exaggerated perspective and odd distortions when using a wide-angle lens. These problems tend to be much worse when using a wide-angle lens for close-ups.

Digital zoom

In the current context there is usually an easy way around the problem. Because the camera will be operating at a much higher resolution than that of the final image, it does not matter if the subject is something less

Photographs for eBay 3

Fig.3.16 This picture of a gold ring was taken using the camera's Macro setting, and then some cropping was applied

than frame-filling in the initial photograph. If the image is cropped to make the subject as large as possible without clipping occurring, it is likely that the resolution of the cropped photograph will still be higher than the minimum needed for an eBay listing. Much the same effect can normally be obtained by using the camera in one of its lower resolution modes and using the digital zoom facility to zoom-in closer. These methods will give much better results than getting too close for the lens to focus properly, or settling for a wide-angle close-up that gives a very distorted and odd looking image.

The photograph of a gold ring shown in Figure 3.16 was taken using the macro mode of the camera, a slightly telephoto zoom setting, and some cropping of the final image to give a digital zoom effect. Photographing something small and highly reflective such as a gold ring is very difficult, but this shot, which was taken with my 99 pence eBay camera, has turned out reasonably well. With anything of this type it tends to look its best if you can find someone suitably elegant to wear it.

Fig.3.17 The subject is too small and little detail can be seen

Fill the frame

Note that it is important to have the subject as large as possible, or something quite close to it. With the modest resolution used for normal eBay pictures, even a frame filling shot will not contain a great deal of detail. With the main subject covering (say) 120 by 180 pixels and a lot of unused background area in the picture, any useful detail might be lost completely. Potential buyers might conclude that you are trying to hide something and they could be put off placing a worthwhile bid. Figure 3.17 shows how not to do it, and Figure 3.18 shows a frame-filling shot that would give potential buyers a good idea of what the object actually looks like. With attractive items, a frame-filling shot has much more impact and helps to show items at their best.

Keep it clean

It is important that any item you put up for sale on eBay should be free from dust and looking at its best, but it is especially important with small objects. Dust that is not apparent when looking at an object can be very apparent in a close-up photograph. The closer up the photograph, the more obvious any specks of dust are likely to become. Try to get small objects free from dust before starting to photograph them, and if dust is apparent in the photographs, clean the objects and redo the photographs.

Photographs for eBay   3

Fig.3.18 A frame-filling shot is much better

Correct focus

The sophisticated electronics in modern cameras has greatly reduced the number of duff photographs due to inaccurate focusing and exposure errors, but it has by no means eliminated them. There are two main causes of pictures being out of focus, and one of these is that the camera cannot focus properly if it is positioned too close to the subject. As pointed out previously, most modern cameras have a macro mode for taking close-up shots, and this facility will often be needed when taking the photographs for eBay listings. Bear in mind that there will still be a limit on how close you can go while still obtaining sharp results.

The other main cause of problems is that the auto-focusing of a camera needs some fine detail with reasonable contrast in order to work properly. This can cause problems when photographing something that has plain surfaces. Some cameras will not actually allow a photograph to be taken unless the auto-focusing has found something it can latch onto, but others will carry on regardless and produce fuzzy pictures. However, there will usually be some form of indicator that lets you know a problem has occurred. Where a camera has the option of using a small area in the middle of the frame, or a much larger area, using this second option increases the chances of the auto-focusing finding something to focus on.

If your camera can only use the centre of the frame for auto-focusing there is a simply ploy that will usually give good results. With most digital cameras the focusing is activated by pressing the shutter button half way down. It is then locked at that setting until the button is fully depressed and the picture is taken. You can therefore get the camera to focus properly by placing any suitable part of the subject at the centre of the frame, pressing the shutter button half way down, waiting for the auto-focusing to operate, framing the subject, and then pressing the shutter all the way down.

Correct exposure

Obtaining accurate exposures is not usually too difficult, and the auto-exposure systems of modern cameras can handle most situations. However, there are some circumstances that can cause problems. Objects that are very light in colour can "fool" automatic exposure systems into producing under exposure, and rather dark pictures. Conversely, very dark objects can come out far too light in the pictures due to over exposure. It is possible to compensate for small amounts of over and under exposure using a photo editing program, but results are generally best if you get things right at the taking stage.

Most cameras have an exposure compensation facility that can be used to correct the exposure in awkward situations where exposure problems will otherwise occur. Use positive exposure compensation to make pictures lighter, or the negative variety to make them darker. With black objects, or those that are very dark in colour, it can be advantageous to use a small amount of over exposure. With a technically correct exposure you can end up with a picture of a black blob that is not recognisable as anything at all! A small amount of over exposure can bring out some detail in the picture and produce something that is a better representation of the object. Only use a small amount of over exposure though, or you could end up with a photograph that makes the object look a bit battered and worn.

Flash compensation

Using the camera's built-in flashgun is a common cause of under exposure. As pointed out previously, shiny surfaces tend to reflect the light from the flashgun back to the camera. These reflections produce very bright highlights that tend to "fool" the automatic exposure system into producing under exposure. In an extreme case you end up with a picture that is white in the highlight areas but is otherwise black. Also as pointed out previously, photographing objects at an angle rather than square-on will usually eliminate large reflections. This should help to reduce problems with under exposure, and might well give a better composed photograph as well.

With really awkward subjects it might be necessary to use exposure compensation in order to obtain good results. Most cameras have an exposure compensation facility that will work when using the built-in flashgun, but this may be separate from the normal exposure compensation facility. Flash and available light exposures are normally handled in different ways. The exposure is usually controlled via the iris mechanism in the lens and by varying the shutter speed. Normally a fairly fast shutter speed is set when using the flashgun, and the exposure is then controlled via the iris mechanism and the power setting of the flashgun. Anyway, if using the normal exposure compensation facility proves ineffective it will be necessary to consult the camera's instruction manual to see how flash exposures can be adjusted.

How many pictures?

The first picture in a listing is included free, but a small additional fee has to be paid for any further pictures. Note that this fee is doubled if an item is listed in two categories. The cost of including extra photographs is minimal compared to the value of expensive items, but with very low cost items you could potentially pay more in fees than you would actually receive from the sale! Also, with some things you can give potential buyers a much better idea of what the item looks like by using half a dozen or more photographs, while one or two photographs can be perfectly adequate with other items. A little common sense has to be exercised here. With something that is fairly expensive and looks quite impressive it could be worthwhile paying extra for using "Supersize" images.

Try to avoid including, and paying for, superfluous photographs. I have seen many eBay listings where several photographs of a group of objects have been provided, but all the photographs were general shots of the group that looked much the same. There is no point in using additional photographs that provide no more information than the first one. With an auction lot that consists of a main item plus some accessories it is a good idea to include a general shot that shows everything that is up for sale. Try to group the objects very close together so that each one is reasonably large in the photograph. However, it is still a good idea to include one or two shots showing the main item in more detail. For example, when selling a camera you could use a general shot showing the camera together with any included accessories such as the battery charger and instruction manual. Close-up shots showing front and rear views of just the camera would then be added to show potential buyers the condition of the main item.

The right one

Strangely, some eBay listings have one or more photographs, but none of them actually show the main item for sale, or it perhaps appears in one photograph where it is about the size of an average full stop! I have seen plenty of listings that show the box everything comes in, but there are no actual pictures of its contents. In some cases there are several different pictures of the box taken from different angles, but still no pictures of its contents. Others show lots of photographs of the box and minor accessories that are of little interest or value, but the main item is nowhere to be seen.

In the photographs you should always give primacy to the item of greatest value, or where appropriate, the items of greatest value. Any box or accessories should be included in at least one photograph, but prominence should be given to the item or items that are of primary interest to potential buyers. Try to look at things from the buyer's point of view, and photograph what you would like to see if you were thinking of placing a bid on the goods.

When listing an item, make sure that the right photographs are used. Particularly when listing several similar items, it is easy to get the photographs muddled-up so that the pictures used do not match the item description and heading. I know, because I have made this mistake on more than one occasion. It can be corrected using the listing editing facilities provided you spot the mistake before anyone places a bid. It is possible to add pictures once a bid has been placed, but you cannot remove the erroneous ones. It is probably best to cancel the listing and start from scratch if you cannot correct it properly.

Photographs for eBay

Fig.3.19 An image being cropped using GIMP 2

Processing

Having obtained some good photographs of the items for sale it is likely that most of the pictures would benefit from a certain amount of processing to optimise results. There is insufficient space available here for a detailed description of all the processes involved in picture optimisation, but in most cases a few simple types of processing will suffice. It may be possible to apply some or even all of the processing in-camera, but it will usually be necessary to use an image editing program.

As explained previously, a basic but adequate program of this type is often included with digital cameras, or a free image editing program can be downloaded from the Internet. The bundled photo editing programs vary greatly in their scope and ease of use, as do the programs available as free downloads on the Internet. In general, the more features the software has to offer, the longer it will take before you become proficient at using it. Unless you are prepared to spend a reasonable amount of time learning to use a photo editing program it is better to opt for one of the programs that concentrates on ease of use.

GIMP 2 (Figure 3.19) is available as a free download and is designed to rival professional photo editing programs. It is certainly a very powerful

3 Photographs for eBay

Fig.3.20 An image being edited using Google's Picasa 3

piece of software, but it perhaps goes beyond the needs of an average eBay user. However, it might be worth trying if you favour programs that have a fairly standard Windows user interface that comes complete with the usual menus and toolbars. GIMP 2 can be downloaded from this web site, which also provides detailed information for this program.

http://www.gimp.org/

Google's Picasa 3 (Figure 3.20) is in most respects a less potent program than GIMP 2, but it has a more modern interface that many will find much easier to use. It provides the basic functions needed when editing photographs for use in eBay listings. It also includes a photo library facility which could be very useful, but this part of the program might take half an hour or more scanning your hard disc drive for photographs when the program is run for the first time. Picasa 3 can be downloaded from:

http://picasa.google.com/

Cropping

The importance of frame-filling shots to maximise the available resolution was pointed out previously. Even if you frame the shot well, leaving just a small amount of unused background area, it is likely the main subject will shrink and that there will be substantially more background in evidence when the picture is displayed on a computer. The reason for this is that the viewfinders of cameras, whether optical or electronic, are often designed to show only about 85 to 90 percent of the picture. The main reason for this is that one of the most common errors when taking pictures is to frame the shot too tightly so that important details are lost outside the margins of the photograph. The classic example of this is where someone takes a picture of a group of people, only to discover that the tops of people's heads are absent when the picture is printed.

One way around the problem is to deliberately frame shots a little too tightly in the viewfinder so that the full image is framed correctly. However, this tends to be a bit "hit and miss", and it is usually better to compose the picture normally in the viewfinder and then crop it later. Some cameras have the ability to crop pictures, but it is a task that can be handled more accurately and easily using photo-editing software. Any picture processing software should have a facility that enables images to be accurately cropped. The cropping facility of GIMP 2 is being used in Figure 3.19.

Exposure adjustment

If there are major problems with incorrect exposure it is better to retake the shot using a suitably adjusted exposure, rather than trying to rescue a grossly underexposed or overexposed photograph. It might be worthwhile trying to adjust the image if it is only suffering from minor overexposure, but with anything more than that it is likely that detail will be lost in the highlights. Slight underexposure is not usually a serious problem, and the automatic exposure systems of many digital cameras are deliberately designed to err on the side of underexposure. The reasoning behind this is that even mild overexposure tends to cause a loss of detail in the highlights, whereas shadow detail can usually be rescued when there is slight underexposure.

The way in which adjustments to the brightness, exposure and contrast are handled depends on the photo-editing software in use. Some cameras have an image optimisation facility, as do most photo-editing programs in one form or another. There will often be automated features for adjusting individual aspects of an image, such as contrast, exposure and colour balance. It makes sense to use automated features with images where they work well, but there will inevitably be a fair percentage of photographs where they have little effect or even make things worse. You then have to use the manual alternatives and exercise your own judgement. In general it is best to use no more processing of images than is really necessary.

Shadow/fill-in

Many images in their "raw" state from the camera are slightly on the dark side, and as explained previously, this is often the result of the camera's exposure system deliberately erring on underexposure in order to prevent lost detail in the highlights. The obvious route when manually correcting this problem is to use the brightness control of an image editing process to lighten the picture. This will have the desired effect, but it is also likely to introduce the lost highlight detail that the camera's exposure system was trying to avoid.

Most photo editing programs have an alternative method that lightens the mid-tones and moderately dark parts of the image while leaving the brightest areas unaltered. This brightens the picture and gives a more natural look without causing the highlights to burn out. The terminology varies from one program to another, but it is usually called something like a shadow, exposure, or fill-in control. There might also be a highlight control that can be used to recover detail from the lightest parts of the picture, but this requires some variation in tone in order to bring out lost details. It can be of no help if, as is often the case, the highlights have burned out to pure white.

Off colour

The automatic white-balance controls of modern digital cameras are usually very good, but there can occasionally be problems with photographs having a strong colour cast. It is best if this type of thing can be avoided in the first place, rather than trying to fix it once it has been allowed to occur. The camera might have several preset colour settings, or some form of adjustable colour temperature setting, and it is worth experimenting with any feature of this type to see if it can improve matters.

Avoid using fancy artificial lighting that might be quite trendy and fashionable, but tends to make things look odd colours. Using flash lighting should avoid major problems with colour. So should the use of natural daylight, except when it is close to sunrise or sunset and the light tends to have a strong red-orange content. It should be possible to correct matters if a colour cast cannot be avoided, and any photo editing program should have at least one method of adjusting the colour balance.

Manually setting the correct colour balance is more difficult than one might expect though.

Colour is problematic with items where it is important that the colours in the photographs are very accurate. If someone is buying an item of clothing from you, they will probably expect the item they receive to accurately match the photograph or photographs in the listing. The problem is that a high degree of accuracy cannot really be achieved. Even if you managed to get everything just right so that the colours displayed on your monitor accurately matched an item for sale, the colours displayed on the monitors of prospective buyers would be different. Computer monitors are not all set up to the same standards, and in most cases they are set to give what the user considers to be the best colour balance. The actual settings used could then be "a country mile" away from any standards for colour reproduction.

The perceived colour of objects tends to vary, depending on the lighting conditions. Colours often appear to change when items are moved from an artificially lit area to one in natural light, and they can look more or less vivid when the intensity of the light is changed. The best approach is to get the colours in the photographs reasonably accurate, using an image editor if necessary. Then state clearly in the item descriptions that the colours are for guidance only, and that their accuracy cannot be guaranteed. Use bold type and red lettering to ensure that this warning stands out very clearly from the rest of the description.

Straight and narrow

One of the most common mistakes when taking scenic photographs is to produce a so-called "sloping horizon". In other words, the camera has been held at a slant instead of horizontally, and this gives a slanting horizon in the photographs. Essentially the same thing can happen when photographing small or large objects. In some cases there may be no accurately defined top and bottom, and the angle of the camera will not be important. With other objects even a slight slant can give odd looking results, and could even give prospective buyers the impression that the item for sale has met with a nasty accident!

Where a photograph is clearly suffering from "camera slant" it is advisable to use a photo editor to rotate it to the correct orientation. This is again a feature that should be available from any image editing software. Rotating an image slightly results in it being increased in size, with a thin triangular blank area being added on each side. It must then be cropped slightly to remove these blank areas. It is therefore a good idea to rotate the image before cropping any excess background. Otherwise you will have to crop it twice, and could end up cropping it too tightly.

In addition to being able to rotate images by small amounts, there should be a facility to rotate them in 90 degree steps. Many digital cameras will automatically rotate an image by 90 degrees if you take a vertical (portrait format) photograph instead of the usual horizontal (landscape format) type. Others will simple leave you with a picture that is on its side when viewed on a monitor. I have seen plenty of pictures of this type on eBay, but this type of thing does not create a very good impression. If necessary, manually rotate the picture to the correct orientation using the built-in facility of the camera or an image processing program.

Resizing

The resolution of the images produced by a modern digital camera, even after a certain amount of cropping, will usually be far higher than the normal size used in eBay listings. As explained previously, eBay recommends uploading oversize images at about one thousand pixels or so on the longest dimension. This is still well below the sizes produced by a reasonably modern digital camera. It is not essential to resize your eBay pictures to match these limits, since the eBay system will automatically reduce images to the required size. However, it can be advantageous to do so, and practically every image editing program has a resizing facility.

One advantage of reducing the size of pictures is that it reduces the time taken to upload them to the eBay server. This is especially important if you are using a slow Internet connection such as an ordinary dial-up type. There is also something to be said for reducing the pictures to the appropriate size before carrying out any processing. You will be seeing the photographs more or less as they will appear on the screen when potential buyers view them. Any processing applied should be apposite to the final image. Processing that looks fine on a large image will not necessarily look quite so good once it has been reduced to a much smaller size. Any sharpening should only be added once any other processing has been completed and the image has been reduced to its final size. Use sharpening in moderation as it can exaggerate any slight imperfections in the subject matter.

4

Everyday eBay

Avoiding scams

Some of the more common eBay scams have already been covered in the previous chapters, but there are a few others that new eBay users should be aware of. There used to be a common scam whereby someone would buy something on eBay and then send a fake email that purported to be from PayPal. The email would state that the item had been paid for, and in most cases it would look quite authentic. In fact the fake email would usually be a modified version of a real PayPal email, and it would therefore look very much like the genuine article.

Of course, close scrutiny of the email would show that it had not originated from PayPal, and there would be no matching transaction in the seller's PayPal account. However, many people fell for this scam as they simply took the email at face value and did not check to see if the money had actually been paid into their account. This scam is now much rarer because eBay have introduced little icons on the My eBay pages, and these show how each sale is progressing (Figure 4.1). In the selling section there is one icon to show that the buyer has gone through the eBay checkout system, and another to show that payment has been made.

Fig.4.1 A set of four icons show how a sale is progressing

On the face of it, PayPal payment has been made if the appropriate icon is present in an item's entry in the My eBay page. This is not necessarily the case if you accept some other form of payment such as a cheque. It might then simply indicate that the buyer has marked the item as "payment sent" in their eBay page. Brief details of how the payment was made should appear if you place the cursor over the payment icon. In the example of Figure 4.1 the item has indeed been paid for using PayPal. Do not jump to conclusions if the My eBay page indicates that an item has been paid for. Either use the cursor to check that the payment has been made using PayPal, or check that the transaction is present in your PayPal account.

When to send

Whether payment is made via PayPal or some other method, always get the payment first and send the goods second. You are almost certainly dealing with a scammer if they try to persuade you to send the goods before payment is made, or before it has cleared in the case of a cheque or similar method of payment. The best course of action with this type of thing is to report it to eBay and cease answering the buyer's messages.

Cash on collection

It is necessary to be a little wary if you accept cash on collection. This is an attractive payment method as it is quick and easy, and it avoids the payment of any fees to PayPal. Unfortunately, buying second-hand items from private buyers using counterfeit money is a popular way of laundering fake cash. Shops mostly train their staff to spot suspicious bank notes and have equipment that can detect forgeries. Private sellers are less likely to spot anything that is not quite right, and are unlikely to have any equipment for checking suspected forgeries. This makes them prime targets for villains. Except with low value items, it is probably best not to accept cash as a method of payment, even if you accept personal collection of items. PayPal is a much safer option.

Money transfer

Never buy anything on eBay using some form of instant money transfer to make the payment. These payment methods are no longer allowed on eBay, but you might find that a seller tries to persuade you to use one instead of paying via PayPal. The problem with an instant money transfer to someone that you do not know is that it is easy for them to collect the cash in some far off country and then never be heard from again. You will be breaking the eBay rules if you use this payment method, and your chances of receiving the goods will be practically non-existent.

Feedback blackmail

A small minority of buyers will buy an item on eBay and then start finding fault with it and attempt to negotiate a lower price with the seller. If the buyer refuses to give a partial refund they will then threaten to leave negative feedback for the seller, together with low seller ratings. This is known as "feedback blackmail", and is really a form of extortion. Where a buyer is genuinely unhappy with some aspect of an item they might be entitled to return it for a full refund, but negotiating a partial refund is not really the eBay way of doing things. It is advisable for sellers to assume a "take it or leave it" stance, and to report any attempts at feedback blackmail to eBay.

eBay phishing

Phishing is a potentially very costly scam where an email is received from a financial organisation of some kind. PayPal was probably the first to be targeted, but several online banks were targeted later, and there can now be few financial companies operating online that have not been the objective of this scam. The email asks you to sign in at the site and confirm your password and other details. The email, superficially at any rate, usually looks very authentic. There is a link on the email that leads to what looks very much like the financial institution's real site, and the address is very similar to the real thing. However, the link actually leads to a fake site where you give away your account details if you sign in and provide the requested information.

So far this scam has not been particularly successful in terms of the number of people who have fallen victim to it. Most recipients of the emails realised that there was something amiss and either ignored or reported it. Others ignored the link and went to the relevant page in the usual way, thus avoiding the fake site. Most of the emails are sent to people who do not have an account with the company concerned! Although only a small percentage of recipients are fooled, each successful attempt to steal account details tends to lead to hundreds or even thousands of pounds being stolen from the account. The total amount stolen using phishing scams must now be immense.

To avoid anything of this type it is just a matter of not supplying passwords or any other sensitive information in answer to emails or telephone calls. As many online organisations go to great lengths to point out, they will never ask you for your password. emails from PayPal and eBay will have your name somewhere near the top, and not just your user ID. If your name is not present on the email, then it is not from PayPal or eBay. Never use links on emails that might be fakes. The links may well take you to an authentic looking site, but like the email, it will also be a fake. Always go to PayPal and eBay using your normal method of accessing them. Ideally, links on emails should never be used, no matter how authentic the emails might appear. Accessing sites in the normal way is much safer.

Spoof eBay emails

I have received numerous spoof eBay emails, but they have not been what could accurately be called phishing emails. They are not sent in an attempt to steal account information. At one time it was quite normal to receive fake eBay emails that were of the standard phishing variety. In order to improve security, changes were made to the way that eBay operates, and this made it harder for thieves and fraudsters to make effective use of hijacked eBay accounts.

It is possible that there are still people who try to hijack eBay accounts, but most of the spoof eBay emails now seem to have a different purpose. The spoof email usually purports to come from someone who has traded with you, and there will usually be some rather vague text asking why an item has not been received or something of this nature. The general idea behind the email is to entice the recipient to operate one of the links in the email. This might just lead to something like a porn or gambling site where you will be invited to join, but more usually it leads to an attack site that will try to infect your computer with some form of malicious software. As usual with anything of this type, the best defence is not to use links on any emails. Frankly, with this type of email it should be pretty obvious that it is a fake. It will not contain your name, and it will refer to an item that you have never bought or sold.

The box

This is not really a scam, and it occurs where the buyer has not bothered to read the item description. They obtain what they think is a real bargain, but when the item arrives they discover that they have bought an empty box! As pointed out in Chapter 2, some items sell at a higher price if they come complete with their original box and inner packing. Many collectors prefer to have items complete with a matching box, and will happily buy a suitable box on eBay.

The buying and selling of empty boxes on eBay is perfectly legitimate provided the listing makes it clear that the box is all you are getting, and that the item it originally contained is not included. It is up to potential buyers to make sure that they read the item description and determine exactly what is on offer before they place a bid or use the Buy-it-Now button. You may not be able to return the item for a refund if the item you obtain matches the item description. Even where the seller will accept the return of the item, paying for both sets of postage will be the buyer's responsibility.

Fake feedback

A problem for anyone setting up an eBay account for fraudulent purposes is that it will start with zero feedback. An offer that looks too good to be true is likely to be ignored if it originates from an eBay account that was set up the day before and has zero feedback. It is likely to be taken more seriously and snare a few victims if it comes from an account that has plenty of good feedback and was set up at least a few months previously. Some fraudsters will therefore set up an account and gradually build up some good feedback before using it for fraudulent purposes.

Fortunately, there are usually some tell-tale signs that all is not well with an account of this type. The fraudster is unlikely to spend large amounts of time and money building up an account that genuinely has a good track record, and will instead take one or two shortcuts. One way of doing this is to buy lots of low-cost items such as light bulbs, stamps, EBooks and guides, or flower seeds. In some cases the fraudster might actually buy goods from legitimate eBay sellers in order to build up some genuine feedback, but it is suspicious if a buyer never seems to end up with anything costing more than a matter of pence.

Often the feedback is totally faked. The fraudster sets up several accounts and then trades between these accounts so that he or she can write their own feedback. The feedback for each account then originates from only a few accounts, whereas there would normally be only a limited amount of repeat business per account. Some fraudsters try to hide this by using private listings that do not divulge the eBay IDs when feedback is viewed. However, this is perhaps even more suspicious, because all or most of the transactions are then via private listings. Typically, only perhaps one or two percent of transactions are made using private listings.

It is also suspicious if an account has only been used to buy and (or) sell an assortment of relatively low value items, there is a long period of inactivity, and then the account is used to sell numerous expensive items such as professional cameras, video equipment, and electronic musical instruments. Everything might be above board, but this can indicate that an account has been hijacked, or purchased from its legitimate owner who will claim that it has been misappropriated. Where the seller's feedback looks in any way suspicious it is advisable to steer well clear of their great offers. You might be missing a bargain, but it is more likely that you are avoiding a great deal of trouble and frustration.

Short duration auctions

Short duration auctions that last one day need to be treated with a certain amount of suspicion. They are not normally a good idea, because relatively few people will see the auction in such a short space of time, leading to a small number of bidders and what is likely to be a low selling price. It could simply be that the person placing the listing genuinely needs to complete the sale and get the money as quickly as possible, and they a prepared to accept a relatively low price.

However, one day auctions have often been used by fraudsters in the past. The fraudster would hijack a legitimate eBay account and then use that account to quickly make as many sales as possible in a short space of time. It was likely that before too long the owner of the account would discover that they had been hoodwinked and would raise the alarm with eBay. The fraudster therefore needed to complete their task and disappear as soon as possible.

This type of thing is now relatively rare because changes in the eBay system have made it difficult for anyone to list goods using a hijacked account. However, this does not stop fraudsters from setting up their own accounts and using them to cheat people. They might still feel the need to obtain some quick sales and then disappear with the money. Therefore, it is always a good idea to look very carefully at any one day auction or Buy-it-Now listing. Be especially wary of Buy-it-Now listings that have a short duration and offer goods at very low prices. Look carefully at the feedback and study the listing for anything suspicious. Remember the old adage that states "if it looks too good to be true, then it almost certainly is".

Dealing off eBay

eBay no longer permits the use of instant money transfers as a payment method, which makes life difficult for the fraudsters as this is their favoured method of payment. With it they can quickly get cash for nonexistent goods, and there is little chance of them getting caught. You need to be very careful if a seller tries to persuade you to use an instant money transfer instead of using PayPal. They will almost certainly be fraudulent traders, and there is little chance of the goods ever being received. Never pay for an eBay transaction using any form of instant money transfer.

Various approaches are used when attempting to persuade buyers to pay by money transfer. One approach is to have a notice in the listing that asks buyers to email the seller using the address provided before making a bid or using the Buy-it-Now button. Using as much guile as they can muster, the seller then tries to persuade the buyer to deal outside eBay. This method has the potential for selling the same nonexistent item to several gullible eBay users.

Another approach is for the seller to let the auction end normally, but they will immediately send a message through the eBay system, making excuses about their PayPal account giving problems, and they will then ask for an alternative method of payment. Of course, this alternative will be some form of instant money transfer. Since these are not permitted for eBay transactions, the buyer is effectively trading outside eBay if they agree to the suggested method of payment. The buyer then stands little chance of receiving the goods, getting a refund, or obtaining any compensation. Never accept an offer to trade outside eBay, and it is probably best to report the matter to eBay if a seller tries to persuade you to pay using an instant money transfer.

Mystery postage

These days the cost of postage and packing is usually included on listings, and in most cases you know the cost before placing a bid. However, some listings have "freight" as the method of delivery, with no mention of the cost in the listing. With a listing of this type it is advisable not to bid unless the seller will give you a firm quote for the delivery charge. Otherwise you might bid on the item and then find that there is a high delivery charge to be paid. It could be that the item is heavy and (or) expensive, and that a high charge is reasonable. On the other hand, the seller might be trying to make a little extra money by inflating the postage charge. Either way, you need to know the cost of delivery before bidding, so that you can take it into account when calculating your maximum bid.

Problems, problems

Most deals on eBay go through without any difficulties, but it is inevitable that there will be occasional problems if you use eBay a great deal. You are very unlucky if you only do a few trades and run into difficulties. Initially you should try to solve the problem amicably by explaining the problem to the other party as clearly as possible. The eBay messaging system can be used for this purpose, or you can get contact details from eBay if the problem is a complex one and you need to talk to the other party on the telephone. Try to deal with things in a matter of fact manner, and avoid getting abusive even if the other party does so. At the other extreme, do not allow the other party to con you into becoming excessively pally, as this is probably a ploy to help them fob you off with an inadequate solution to the problem.

Your rights as a consumer vary depending on whether you are dealing with a business user or a private eBay user, and whether the item was purchased as a Buy-it-Now item or via an auction. The same is true of your obligations when selling. Looking at things from the buyer's point of view, you have the best protection when purchasing from a business seller via a Buy-it-Now offer, and the least when buying from a private seller via an auction. The terms of the seller might give you more protection than is required by the law of the land. For example, I accept returns on any item if the buyer is at all unhappy with it, whether or not I am required to do so. Unfortunately, most sellers are not as accommodating as this.

Dispute resolution

eBay used to have a policy of laissez-faire, with the buyers and sellers being expected to sort things out amongst themselves. Buyers and sellers are still encouraged to settle their differences by negotiation if at all possible, but there is now an eBay dispute resolution process. Note that as a buyer you will need to pay using PayPal in order to make full use of this process. If you are unable to settle a dispute through negotiation with the other party, or they simply do not respond to your messages, it should be possible to settle things via the eBay dispute process.

Someone at eBay will arbitrate, and if necessary a refund will be provided to the buyer. I have used this system on a few occasions to obtain refunds from so-called "silent sellers". These are sellers who do not send the goods or respond to any messages. Perhaps in this type of case the seller has become ill after placing the listing, or possibly the item did not reach the expected price and they decided not to sell or deal with the buyer in any way. Whatever the cause, you just have to accept that this will happen in a few cases.

Shifting goalposts

A very small minority of sellers will try to change the conditions of the sale after the auction has ended. This is usually in the form of a request for extra postage because they have underestimated the cost of posting the item to you. It is up to you whether you take pity on them, but I would be inclined not to do so. You have based your bid on the total price including postage and packing, and would have presumably bid a little less if the higher postage charge had been quoted on the listing.

It can also work the other way with buyers winning an auction and then trying to negotiate a lower postage charge because they feel that the one quoted is excessive. Many buyers seem to grossly underestimate the cost of sending things through the post. They seem to base their estimate on what it cost them to post a parcel twenty years ago! Assuming the postage charge was included on the listing, the buyer should have known the cost of postage prior to bidding, and you are within your rights to insist on the deal going ahead on the original terms.

Being realistic about matters, it is not really possible to force someone to go ahead with a sale if they are determined not to do so, and with the vast majority of items it is not worth suing them. All you can do is walk away from the deal and report the matter to eBay. Go through the eBay dispute process if they have been paid through PayPal and have not issued a full refund.

Be patient

Once you have made a sale it is only natural to be eager for payment and to complete the deal. Similarly, once you have paid for an item it is only natural to want the goods delivered as soon as possible. Unfortunately, not everyone operates in a fast and efficient manner, and things can sometimes move fairly slowly. Most business sellers on eBay are quite quick, but there are exceptions. Private buyers and sellers are generally slower, but again there are exceptions. When dealing with non-business eBay users it pays to bear in mind that they will probably have plenty of things to do, and eBay is just a small part of their lives.

Try to be patient, and avoid hassling users who deal with things something less than instantly. I generally wait seven days for either the goods to be delivered or the seller to indicate that they are on their way. It is probably best to reduce this period to two or three days for an expensive item. After that time it is reasonable to ask the seller if the goods have been despatched, and to use the eBay dispute process if that fails to elicit a response.

Stick to the rules

Keeping to the eBay rules is something you will expect others to do, but do not forget that it is also up to you to do things "by the book". Describe goods accurately in listings, charge reasonable postage rates, pack items well, send them on time, get a receipt of posting, ensure that expensive items are adequately insured while they are in transit, and deal promptly, courteously and efficiently with any problems that arise. Actually, provided you operate your eBay selling account efficiently and within the rules there should be very few problems to deal with. Be willing to own up if you should make a mistake, and do all that you reasonably can in order to put matters right. Your feedback and detailed seller ratings will suffer if you fail to obey the rules and operate your selling account inefficiently. This will make buyers reluctant to bid on your items, which will therefore tend to sell at low prices. Ultimately, you could even be banned from eBay.

As an eBay buyer you have to do little more than pay promptly and leave feedback when the deal is completed successfully. If things go wrong, try to deal with the seller in an amicable fashion and do not make unreasonable demands. Make a determined attempt to negotiate a reasonable settlement of the problem with the seller, but do not be fobbed off with lame excuses and sob stories. Use the eBay customer support service if you seem to be getting nowhere, and resort to the eBay dispute resolution facility as a last resort rather than a starting point.

My eBay

It is important to become familiar with your My eBay page sooner rather than later, as it is from here that you track and control your eBay activities. The main part of the page contains lists of items in categories such as a watching list, items you are bidding on, items bought and items sold. The sheer quantity of information and the huge number of links can make the My eBay page a bit bewildering at first. By default the Activity page is displayed, but there are three other pages available via four tabs near the top of the page. These are in the middle left-hand section of the

Fig.4.2 Tabs give a choice of four different sets of information

partial page shown in Figure 4.2. The Messages page is an important one, and you need to check the Messages tab periodically. A number will appear next to the word "Messages" if there are new messages to be read. These will be things like queries from prospective buyers about items you are selling, answers to your queries about items you are interested in buying, and system generated messages from eBay.

The Account tab leads to a page where your account information is displayed, and it is possible to change things like your address and telephone number. It is also possible to alter certain preferences, such as when eBay sends system generated emails. With the default settings it is likely that eBay will send you an excessive amount of emails, most of them simply stating the obvious. It is therefore a good idea to alter the email related settings so that only the more important types are sent to you.

The displayed lists have an Actions column, and this provides access to some important features. A default action is shown against each item in a list, but there is also a "More actions" link that provides a range of options via a drop-down menu. The options available depend on the list the item appears in, and the "state of play" with that item. With an item you have bought or sold for instance, there will be the option of leaving feedback if you have not already done so.

For an item that you have sold and posted to the buyer there will be the option of marking it as despatched. It is a good idea to use this one as soon as possible once anything has been sent to the buyer. It switches on the appropriate icon in their list of items bought, so that they can see that the item is on its way to them. With an expensive item I would also recommend sending a message with additional information such as the method of delivery used, expected delivery date, tracking number, or

4 Everyday eBay

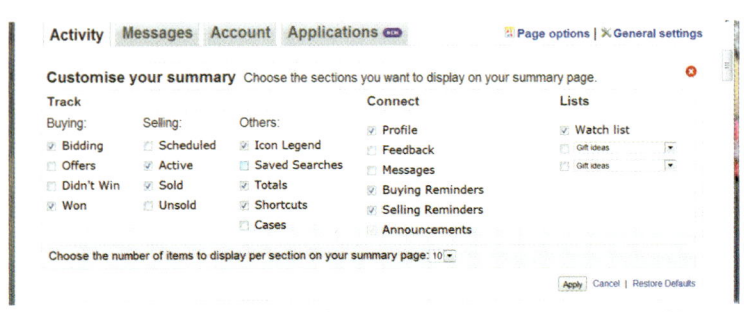

Fig.4.3 The information in the Summary section can be selected here

whatever. It is a good idea to warn buyers if a signature will be required when the item is delivered.

Customise

A degree of customisation is possible with your My eBay page. Operating the Page Option link near the top of the page (see Figure 4.2) produces the pop-up window of Figure 4.3. Here it is possible to select the lists and other information that will be displayed in the Summary section of the page. In order to make the page as easy to use as possible it is a good idea to switch off any sections that are not used fairly often. Any sections that are switched off can still be accessed very quickly using the links in the Summary column down the left-hand side of the My eBay page.

Each list in the main Summary section of the page has an Edit link in the top right-hand corner. This has options to move each list up or down, so you can position the most frequently used lists at the top, and move the less frequently used ones to the bottom section of the page. There is a small palette of colours that enable the colour of the bar at the top of each list to be changed. Using a different colour for each list can make it easier to quickly scroll down the page to the one you require. There is also a Customise option, and this provides some control over the information that will be included in each list, but the inclusion of some fields is mandatory.

Index

A

abroad	46
Action menu	24
alert facility	8
anti-blur	85
automatic exposure	98

B

background	84
background colour	27
backlighting	83
BayGenie	13, 18
Best Match	72
Bidding list	23
bidding sites	28
box	66
brightness	103
browser	8, 19
Buy-it-Now	1, 45, 58, 67
buyer protection	46
buying	1

C

camera	52
camera shake	84
card reader	53
category	45, 69
close-ups	94
colour cast	104
completed listings	67
contrast	88, 103
Control Panel	10
conversion rate	16
cropping	102
currency converter	14
customisation	118
customs duties	46
customs form	80

D

damage	56
dealing off eBay	113
description	47, 56

diffuser	93
digital camera	52
digital zoom	94
dispute	114
distance selling	39
double-image	85

E

E-cheque	39
eBay Help	15
eBay item number	20
eBay toolbars	7
emails	109, 110
ending soonest	72
erasing	74
exposure	98, 103
exposure compensation	98

F

fake email	110
Favourites	35
feedback	45
feedback blackmail	129
fees	63
file shredding	76
fill-in	91, 94, 104
film camera	53
filtered search	70
final value fee	3, 41
Firefox	8, 35
fixed price	108
flash	86
flash compensation	99
flashgun	90
flatbed scanners	54
focus	97
for parts	49
forgeries	108

G

GIMP	81, 101
glare	88
Goofbay	29, 73

119

Index

H

heading	70
Help	15
highlights	84
homepage	34

I

ID	13, 18, 28
image editing	101
image editor	44
image stabiliser	85
inflated prices	65
instruction manuals	66
Internet	5, 11, 22, 28
ISO	86
item number	36

L

language	47
light modifier	93
low start	57

M

macro	94
Make Offer	62
marketing	51
minimum reserve	1
misspelled	74
money transfer	2
My eBay	23, 116

N

| newly listed | 71 |
| not working | 49 |

O

offers	40
one day auction	112
outside eBay	61

P

packing	77
password	13, 18, 28
PayPal	39, 80
personal collection	77
personal data	74
phishing	109
photo processing	43
photograph	42, 51
Picasa	81, 102
postage	2, 8
postage fraud	4

R

rare	60
refund	42, 47
registration	31
reserve	1, 44, 58, 61
resizing	106
rotate	105

S

scams	61
scanning	54
search	8, 59
search types	68
second chance offer	40
selling	51
selling abroad	79
shill bidding	38
sidebars	7
size	56
sniping	5
sniping service	29
software	9
Sort by	71
starting price	57, 61

T

telephoto	82
toolbars	7
translation	47

W

Watch List	23
wide angle	82
wrong category	45